THE VANCOUVER SUN

the best

soups

BY CANADA'S BEST-SELLING AUTHORS FROM *THE VANCOUVER SUN* TEST KITCHEN

RUTH PHELAN AND BRENDA THOMPSON

Published by Pacific Newspaper Group,
A division of Canwest Publishing Inc.
1-200 Granville Street
Vancouver, B.C.
V6C 3N3

Pacific Newspaper Group President and Publisher:
        Kevin Bent

Library and Archives Canada Cataloguing in Publication

Phelan, Ruth, 1960-

        The best soups/
        Ruth Phelan and Brenda Thompson.

Includes index.
ISBN 978-0-9697356-9-4

        1. Soups. I. Thompson, Brenda, 1944-
        II. Title.

TX757.P43 2008   641.8'13   C2008-906263-9

Photos by Kim Stallknecht except: Halibut Saffron Soup, Chicken Noodle Soup with Herbs, Mexican Pumpkin Soup, Roasted Vegetable Soup, Soup Aux Fruits Rouges, by Peter Battistoni.

Edited by Shelley Fralic

Nutritional Analysis by Jean Fremont

Printed and bound in Canada by Friesens

First Edition

10 9 8 7 6 5 4 3 2 1

Introduction

Soup's on!

What other food warms us up or cools us down, chasing away the winter blahs or refreshing us on a warm summer night?

The Best Soups, the seventh in our cookbook series, is loaded with hearty, one-dish home-made soups and savoury accompaniments, developed and tested to perfection in our *Vancouver Sun* Test Kitchen.

Our easy-to-follow recipes include classic soups, seasonal soups, hot and cold soups, and easy, nutritious and quick soups that serve families big and small.

There's a fresh approach to old favourites, like our Chicken Noodle Soup with Fresh Herbs, as well as recipes with enough left over to freeze, like our hearty Old-Fashioned Ham Soup. For entertaining, soups such as our Chilled Strawberry Dessert Soup or Mussels Bathed in Pesto Broth are sure winners.

So get out your best soup pot, and don't forget the croutons.

Ruth Phelan
Brenda Thompson
Vancouver, B.C.
November 2008

A Cook's Guide to the Recipes

- Read the recipe from start to finish before you start to prepare ingredients. Ensure that you have all the ingredients as well as the necessary equipment.

- You can make your own home-made stock or use cartons of ready-to-use stock available in supermarkets. Not all commercial stock, sometimes labelled broth, tastes the same. Experiment and select the best-tasting one you can find.

- Check your local fish shop for fresh or frozen fish stock. We used fish stock (made from halibut bones) that we purchased from our fishmonger. Although we prefer fish soup when it's made with fish stock, you can substitute chicken stock.

- Vegetable stock can be substituted for chicken or beef stock but it will change the flavour of the soup.

- We find the blender does a better job at pureeing soup mixtures resulting in a silky-smooth soup. If you do not have a blender, use a food processor.

- If you prefer a soup with a thinner consistency, simply add a little extra liquid — stock, water or milk — depending on the liquid used in the recipe.

- To freeze soup, transfer cool soup to airtight container and freeze for up to 2 weeks. Let thaw overnight in refrigerator.

- Use medium-size fruit and vegetables unless specified otherwise.

- All recipes use dried pasta unless specified otherwise.

- We use Italian (flat-leaf) parsley but you could substitute curly parsley.

- If fresh herbs are not on hand, use dried herbs but use less — about one-quarter to one-third of the amount.

- We use Hungarian sweet paprika but regular (not hot) paprika could be substituted.

- Buttermilk is 1.5 per cent M.F.

- Milk is 2 per cent M.F. unless specified otherwise.

- Parmesan cheese is freshly grated.

- Pepper is freshly ground.

Halibut Saffron Soup (recipe on following page)

Hot Soups

Halibut Saffron Soup

2	tablespoons (30 mL) extra-virgin olive oil
2	celery stalks, chopped
1	large leek, sliced
1	onion, chopped
1	garlic clove, minced
⅛	teaspoon (0.5 mL) dried crushed hot red pepper
4	cups (1 L) fish stock
1	(796 mL) can diced tomatoes
⅓	cup (75 mL) dry white wine
¼	teaspoon (1 mL) saffron threads, crushed
1	pound (500 g) skinless halibut fillet, cut into 1-inch (2.5 cm) pieces
1	teaspoon (5 mL) fresh lemon juice
½	cup (125 mL) chopped fresh Italian (flat-leaf) parsley
2	teaspoons (10 mL) chopped fresh oregano
	Salt and pepper

In large heavy pot, heat oil over medium-low heat. Add celery, leek, onion, garlic and dried red pepper; saute for 12 minutes or until tender. Add stock, tomatoes, wine and saffron; increase heat to medium-high and bring to a boil. Add halibut; reduce heat and simmer for 3 minutes or until fish flakes easily when tested with a fork. Add lemon juice, parsley and oregano. Add salt and pepper to taste.

Tips

• *Prawn and Halibut variation: Decrease halibut to ¾ pound (350 g). Add ½ pound (250 g) shelled and deveined raw prawns when adding halibut.*
• *You can substitute cod for halibut.*
• *Saffron is one of the most expensive spices but fortunately very little is needed to season a dish. It imparts a very distinctive flavour (there's nothing else that tastes quite like it) and an intense yellow colour to any dish it's added to.*

Makes 6 servings. PER SERVING: 197 cal, 19 g pro, 7 g fat, 14 g carb.

Speedy Snapper Soup

1	tablespoon (15 mL) extra-virgin olive oil
2	carrots, diced
2	celery stalks, sliced
1	small onion, chopped
3	cups (750 mL) fish or chicken stock
2	(398 mL) cans stewed tomatoes
1	large potato, cut into 1-inch (2.5 cm) pieces
1	pound (500 g) snapper fillets, cut into 1-inch (2.5 cm) pieces
2	cups (500 mL) coarsely chopped fresh spinach
¼	cup (50 mL) chopped fresh Italian (flat-leaf) parsley
	Salt and pepper

In large heavy pot, heat oil over medium-high heat. Add carrots, celery and onion; saute for 4 minutes or until onion is tender. Add stock, stewed tomatoes and potato; increase heat to high and bring to a boil. Reduce heat and simmer, covered, for 10 minutes or until potato is almost tender. Add snapper; simmer, uncovered, for 3 minutes. Add spinach and parsley; cook for 2 minutes or until fish flakes easily when tested with a fork. Add salt and pepper to taste.

Tips
• For convenience, purchase washed, ready-to-use spinach.
A 283-gram package yields about 12 cups (3 L) lightly packed.
• If desired, substitute your favourite white fish such as cod or halibut in place of the snapper.
• To ensure complete removal of bones from fish fillet, lay fillet on work surface and gently rub fingers over the entire flesh surface; if you detect a bone, remove it with tweezers.

Makes 4 servings. PER SERVING: 306 cal, 34 g pro, 7 g fat, 29 g carb.

Salmon and Wild Rice Soup

1 tablespoon (15 mL) butter, at room temperature
1 tablespoon (15 mL) extra-virgin olive oil
1 celery stalk, diced
1 leek, sliced thin
1 cup (250 mL) sliced, stemmed shiitake mushrooms
¼ cup (50 mL) dry white wine
2 tablespoons (30 mL) all-purpose flour
4 cups (1 L) fish stock
1 bay leaf
¾ pound (350 g) skinless salmon fillet, cut into 1-inch (2.5 cm) pieces
¾ cup (175 mL) cream (10 per cent M.F.)
½ cup (125 mL) regular wild rice (not toasted), cooked
1 teaspoon (5 mL) fresh lemon juice
¼ cup (50 mL) chopped fresh Italian (flat-leaf) parsley
Salt and pepper

In large heavy pot, heat butter and oil over medium heat. Add celery, leek and mushrooms; saute for 5 minutes or until tender. Add wine; cook for 1 minute. Sprinkle vegetables with flour; cook for 1 minute, stirring constantly. Gradually stir in stock. Add bay leaf; increase heat to medium-high and bring to a boil, stirring occasionally. Add salmon; reduce heat and simmer for 1 minute. Add cream and cooked rice; cook for 2 minutes or until fish flakes easily when tested with a fork (do not boil). Discard bay leaf. Add lemon juice and parsley. Add salt and pepper to taste.

Tip: To cook wild rice, place ½ cup (125 mL) rice and 2½ cups (625 mL) cold water in large heavy saucepan. Place over high heat and bring to a boil. Reduce heat and simmer, covered, for 45 minutes or until rice is tender; drain.

Makes 4 servings. PER SERVING: 320 cal, 22 g pro, 17 g fat, 20 g carb.

Snapper and Potato Chowder

1	tablespoon (15 mL) extra-virgin olive oil
3	bacon strips, chopped
2	celery stalks, diced
1	onion, chopped
1	small red bell pepper, diced
4	cups (1 L) fish or chicken stock
3	cups (750 mL) milk (1 per cent M.F.)
1	teaspoon (5 mL) chopped fresh thyme
1	pound (500 g) snapper fillets, cut into 1-inch (2.5 cm) pieces
1½	cups (375 mL) instant potato flakes
1	(341 mL) can whole kernel corn, drained
1	teaspoon (5 mL) finely grated lemon zest
	Salt and pepper
2	green onions, chopped

In large heavy pot, heat oil over medium-high heat. Add bacon; saute for 3 minutes or until crisp. With slotted spoon, remove bacon.

Add celery and onion to pot; saute for 3 minutes. Add bell pepper; saute for 2 minutes or until bell pepper is tender-crisp. Add stock, milk, thyme and bacon; increase heat to high and bring just to a boil. Add snapper; reduce heat and simmer for 3 to 5 minutes or until fish flakes easily when tested with a fork. Remove from heat; stir in potato flakes, corn, zest, 1 teaspoon (5 mL) salt and ½ teaspoon (2 mL) pepper. Return to heat and stir constantly until hot and slightly thickened. Add green onions. Add salt and pepper to taste.

Tip: Instant mashed potato flakes thicken this soup, avoiding the common addition of cream with its extra fat. They're a handy pantry item (supermarkets usually stock them alongside other dried potato products).

Makes 4 servings. PER SERVING: 472 cal, 38 g pro, 18 g fat, 42 g carb.

Fennel, Black Bean and Tuna Soup

2   tablespoons (30 mL) extra-virgin olive oil
1   small fennel bulb, trimmed, cored and chopped
1   small onion, chopped
2   garlic cloves, minced
1   (796 mL) can stewed tomatoes
1½ cups (375 mL) bottled clam juice
1   (540 mL) can black beans, drained and rinsed
1   (170 g) can solid white tuna (packed in water), drained and
    separated into small chunks
½   cup (125 mL) chopped fresh Italian (flat-leaf) parsley
1   tablespoon (15 mL) chopped fresh basil
1   tablespoon (15 mL) chopped fresh oregano
    Salt and pepper

In large heavy pot, heat oil over medium heat. Add fennel, onion and garlic; saute for 10 minutes or until tender. Add stewed tomatoes and clam juice; bring to a boil. Add beans, tuna, parsley, basil and oregano; reduce heat and simmer for 2 minutes or until heated through. Add salt and pepper to taste.

Tips

• Raw or cooked, fennel contributes a delicate, slightly sweet licorice taste to dishes. Avoid buying fennel with flowering fronds — it's old. To prepare fennel, remove stalks, fronds and any brown outer leaves. (Fronds can be used as an anise-flavoured herb.) Cut fennel in half or quarters depending on size then cut into slices and chop.
• Fish stock can be substituted for clam juice.

Makes 4 servings. PER SERVING: 318 cal, 21 g pro, 8 g fat, 43 g carb.

Clam and Corn Chowder

1	cup (250 mL) bottled clam juice
4	pounds (2 kg) littleneck or manila clams, scrubbed
¼	pound (125 g) sliced pancetta, chopped coarse
2	celery stalks, sliced thin
1	onion, chopped
2	tablespoons (30 mL) all-purpose flour
3	cups (750 mL) milk
2	Yukon Gold potatoes, cut into ½-inch (1 cm) cubes
1	bay leaf
	Fresh thyme sprig
1	(398 mL) can whole kernel corn, drained
½	cup (125 mL) chopped fresh Italian (flat-leaf) parsley
	Salt and pepper

In large heavy pot, bring clam juice to a boil over medium-high heat. Add clams; cover, reduce heat slightly and steam for 5 to 8 minutes or until clams open. (Discard any clams that do not open.) Remove clam meat from shells and place meat in bowl, reserving a few clams in shells for garnish. Reserve clam juice in pot. Line a fine-mesh sieve with double thickness of dampened cheesecloth and set over bowl. Strain reserved juice in pot through sieve and measure 2 cups (500 mL); set aside.

In large heavy pot, saute pancetta over medium heat for 4 minutes or until just beginning to crisp. Add celery and onion; saute for 5 minutes or until tender. Reduce heat to low. Sprinkle vegetables and pancetta with flour; cook for 2 minutes, stirring constantly. Gradually whisk in milk and 2 cups (500 mL) strained clam juice. Add potatoes, bay leaf and thyme; increase heat to medium-high and bring to a simmer, stirring occasionally. Reduce heat and simmer for 10 minutes or until potatoes are tender. Discard bay leaf and thyme sprig. Add corn, parsley, reserved clam meat and clams in their shells to soup; place over medium-low heat and heat through (do not boil). Add salt and pepper to taste.

Makes 6 servings. PER SERVING: 323 cal, 25 g pro, 11 g fat, 33 g carb.

Mussels Bathed in Pesto Broth

4	tablespoons (60 mL) butter, at room temperature (divided)
1	tablespoon (15 mL) extra-virgin olive oil
½	cup (125 mL) finely chopped shallots
3	garlic cloves, minced
1	cup (250 mL) fish stock
1	cup (250 mL) dry white wine
½	cup (125 mL) chopped fresh Italian (flat-leaf) parsley, divided
4	pounds (2 kg) mussels, scrubbed and debearded
2	tablespoons (30 mL) store-bought or home-made fresh pesto
1	teaspoon (5 mL) fresh lemon juice
	Salt and pepper
	Garlic Croutes (see recipe, page 87)

In large heavy pot, heat 1 tablespoon (15 mL) butter and oil over medium heat. Add shallots and garlic; saute for 4 minutes or until tender. Add stock, wine, ¼ cup (50 mL) parsley and remaining 3 tablespoons (45 mL) butter; simmer for 4 minutes. Increase heat to medium-high. Add mussels; cover and steam for 4 to 5 minutes or until they open, shaking pot occasionally so they cook evenly. (Discard any mussels that do not open.) Add pesto and lemon juice to pot. Add remaining ¼ cup (50 mL) parsley. Add salt and pepper to taste.

Divide mussels and stock mixture among 8 serving bowls. Serve 2 croutes with each serving.

Tips

• *Select mussels with tightly closed shells that are void of cracks and are not broken. Tap any mussels that are open — if they close promptly they're safe to use. Discard any that remain open.*

• *To clean mussels, scrub shells under cold running water. To remove beards (fibrous tufts near hinge of shell) give them a firm tug. The best tool for this job is a rounded paring knife or small blunt-nosed pliers.*

Makes 8 servings. PER SERVING: 349 cal, 21 g pro, 17 g fat, 22 g carb.

Malaysian Prawn Soup

6½	ounces (200 g) cellophane (bean thread) noodles
1	tablespoon (15 mL) extra-virgin olive oil
⅓	cup (75 mL) minced shallots
3	garlic cloves, minced
2	tablespoons (30 mL) grated fresh ginger
2	Thai red peppers, seeded, deveined and minced
1½	teaspoons (7 mL) ground turmeric
3	cups (750 mL) chicken stock
1	(400 mL) can regular (not light) coconut milk, stirred
1	teaspoon (5 mL) finely grated lime zest
2	tablespoons (30 mL) fresh lime juice
20	shelled and deveined raw prawns
	Salt and pepper
1	cup (250 mL) each watercress sprigs and bean sprouts
2	tablespoons (30 mL) chopped fresh cilantro
2	green onions, julienned
4	lime wedges

Bring large pot of water to a boil; remove from heat. Add noodles and let soak for 10 minutes or until tender; drain and set aside.

Meanwhile, heat oil in large non-stick frypan over medium heat. Add shallots, garlic, ginger, red peppers and turmeric; saute for 3 minutes, stirring constantly. Add stock, coconut milk, and lime zest and juice; increase heat to medium-high and bring to a boil. Reduce heat and simmer for 3 minutes. Add prawns; simmer for 5 minutes or until prawns are pink. Add salt and pepper to taste.

Put an equal portion of noodles, watercress and sprouts in each of 4 bowls. Add an equal portion of hot soup to each bowl. Top each serving with a sprinkling of cilantro and green onions, and a lime wedge.

Tip: *Use regular coconut milk; light coconut milk will curdle slightly.*

Makes 4 servings. PER SERVING: 486 cal, 15 g pro, 26 g fat, 53 g carb.

Chop-Chop Cioppino

2	tablespoons (30 mL) extra-virgin olive oil
1	small fennel bulb, trimmed, cored and chopped
1	small onion, chopped
3	garlic cloves, minced
3	canned anchovy fillets
3½	cups (875 mL) fish or chicken stock
1	(540 mL) can tomatoes (undrained), chopped
1	pound (500 g) skinless cod or halibut fillets, cut into 1½-inch (4 cm) pieces
12	littleneck or manila clams, scrubbed
12	shelled and deveined raw prawns
	Salt and pepper

In large heavy pot, heat oil over medium heat. Add fennel, onion, garlic and anchovy fillets; saute for 10 minutes or until vegetables are tender. Add stock and tomatoes; bring to a boil. Add cod; reduce heat and simmer for 2 minutes. Add clams and prawns; simmer for 3 to 5 minutes or until prawns are pink, clams are open and cod can be easily flaked with a fork. (Discard any clams that do not open.) Add salt and pepper to taste.

Tips

• *Be sure to prepare the cod, clams and prawns while the vegetables are cooking. The clams and prawns have to be ready to add to the soup 2 minutes after the cod is added to the pot.*

• *Use scissors to chop canned tomatoes right in the can. You'll save a little time and a lot of cleanup.*

Makes 4 servings. PER SERVING: 286 cal, 37 g pro, 10 g fat, 10 g carb.

Turkey Tortilla Soup

1	tablespoon (15 mL) extra-virgin olive oil
1	onion, chopped
2	garlic cloves, minced
1	teaspoon (5 mL) chili powder
7	cups (1.75 L) chicken stock
1	(398 mL) can stewed tomatoes
1	(398 mL) can red kidney or black beans, drained and rinsed
1	(199 mL) can whole kernel corn, drained
2	cups (500 mL) diced cooked turkey breast
1	cup (250 mL) coarsely broken, lightly salted corn tortilla chips
¼	teaspoon (1 mL) chipotle or other hot pepper sauce
2	teaspoons (10 mL) fresh lime juice
	Salt and pepper
	Light sour cream
	Chopped fresh cilantro

In large heavy pot, heat oil over medium-high heat. Add onion and garlic; saute for 3 minutes or until tender. Add chili powder; cook for 1 minute, stirring constantly. Add stock, stewed tomatoes, beans, corn, turkey, chips and hot sauce; increase heat to high and bring to a boil. Reduce heat and simmer for 1 minute. Add lime juice. Add salt and pepper to taste. Top each serving with a dollop of sour cream and a sprinkling of cilantro.

Tips
• *We used slightly salted chips. Select your favourite brand of tortilla chips and then adjust how much salt you add to the soup accordingly.*
• *Just a spoonful or two of this heart-warming midweek soup will have you dreaming of a warm Mexican beach. It's spicy, robust and, yes, we added tortilla chips to the soup — they didn't just fall in. Real chili-heads will want to increase the hot pepper sauce to taste.*

Makes 5 servings. PER SERVING: 329 cal, 30 g pro, 9 g fat, 33 g carb.

Turkey and Wheat Berry Soup

1½	cups (375 mL) hard wheat berries, rinsed
2	tablespoons (30 mL) extra-virgin olive oil
5	large carrots, diced
3	celery stalks, chopped
2	onions, chopped
2	garlic cloves, minced
10	cups (2.5 L) chicken stock
½	teaspoon (2 mL) each salt and pepper
½	teaspoon (2 mL) dried rosemary leaves, crushed
1	bay leaf
1	(540 mL) can stewed tomatoes (undrained), chopped
1	(540 mL) can chickpeas, drained and rinsed
4	cups (1 L) coarsely chopped chard, optional
3	cups (750 mL) cubed cooked turkey breast
1	tablespoon (15 mL) fresh lemon juice
½	cup (125 mL) chopped fresh Italian (flat-leaf) parsley
½	cup (125 mL) grated parmesan cheese

Put berries in large bowl; cover with 4 cups (1 L) water. Let stand overnight; drain and set aside.

In large heavy pot, heat oil over medium-high heat. Add carrots, celery, onions and garlic; saute for 8 minutes or until onion is tender. Add stock, drained berries, salt, pepper, rosemary and bay leaf; cover and bring to a boil. Reduce heat and simmer for 35 minutes or until berries are just tender and chewy. (Once the berries start to split, stop cooking.) Add stewed tomatoes, chickpeas, chard and turkey; increase heat, simmer, covered, for 5 minutes or until chard is tender. Discard bay leaf. Add lemon juice and parsley. *(To freeze, see page 4.)* Top each serving with 1 tablespoon (15 mL) parmesan cheese.

Tip: Look for hard wheat berries (kernels) at natural food stores.

Makes 8 servings. PER SERVING: 423 cal, 29 g pro, 10 g fat, 57 g carb.

Chicken Noodle Soup with Herbs

2	tablespoons (30 mL) extra-virgin olive oil
2	leeks, sliced thin
1	cup (250 mL) sliced mushrooms
8	cups (2 L) chicken stock
2	carrots, sliced
2	celery stalks, sliced
2	cups (500 mL) broad noodles
½	pound (250 g) boneless skinless chicken thighs, cut into ½-inch (1 cm) pieces
¼	pound (125 g) snow peas, trimmed and cut diagonally into thirds
1	tablespoon (15 mL) chopped fresh rosemary
2	teaspoons (10 mL) chopped fresh thyme
	Salt and pepper

In large heavy pot, heat oil over medium-high heat. Add leeks and mushrooms; saute for 2 minutes. Add stock; bring to a boil. Add carrots and celery; cook, covered, for 6 minutes.

Add noodles to stock mixture and boil, uncovered, for 4 minutes. Add chicken, snow peas, rosemary and thyme; bring to a boil. Reduce heat and simmer for 3 minutes or until chicken is cooked, and noodles and vegetables are tender. Add salt and pepper to taste.
(To freeze, see page 4.)

Tip: *For convenience, buy packaged sliced mushrooms. They're not washed, so you'll have to rinse them with cold water and pat dry with paper towel to remove excess moisture.*

Makes 4 servings. PER SERVING: 287 cal, 18 g pro, 11 g fat, 30 g carb.

Big Batch Beef Vegetable Soup

1	tablespoon (15 mL) extra-virgin olive oil
1	pound (500 g) lean ground beef
1	large onion, chopped
4	garlic cloves, minced
8	cups (2 L) beef stock
1	(398 mL) can stewed tomatoes (undrained), chopped
2	tablespoons (30 mL) herbs and spices tomato paste
4	carrots, sliced very thin
2	celery stalks, sliced thin
¾	cup (175 mL) tiny pasta rings or stars
1	(398 mL) can navy beans, drained and rinsed
½	cup (125 mL) chopped fresh Italian (flat-leaf) parsley
	Salt and pepper

In large heavy pot, heat oil over medium heat. Add beef, onion and garlic; saute for 12 minutes or until beef is no longer pink and onion is tender, breaking beef up with spoon and stirring frequently. Drain off fat.

Add stock, stewed tomatoes and tomato paste to beef mixture. Increase heat to high, cover and bring to a boil. Add carrots and celery; cover and bring to a boil. Add pasta; reduce heat and boil gently, uncovered, for 5 minutes or until pasta is almost tender, stirring occasionally. Add beans; cook for 2 minutes or until pasta is tender. Add parsley. Add salt and pepper to taste. *(To freeze, see page 4.)*

Tips
• *A tasty substitution for the beef is extra-lean ground bison.*
• *Tomato paste is now available with a variety of seasonings. We used one seasoned with herbs and spices as a short cut to boost flavour.*
• *To drain fat from pot, tilt pot, push meat to one side and press with back of spoon to release more fat, then use a turkey baster to remove and discard fat.*

Makes 12 servings. PER SERVING: 145 cal, 12 g pro, 2 g fat, 19 g carb.

Chili Soup

1	tablespoon (15 mL) extra-virgin olive oil
1	pound (500 g) lean ground beef
1	large onion, chopped
4	garlic cloves, minced
1	large green bell pepper, chopped
1½	cups (375 mL) beef stock
2	(540 mL) cans stewed tomatoes with chili seasonings (undrained), chopped
¼	cup (50 mL) chopped, drained sun-dried tomatoes (oil-packed)
2	bay leaves
1	(540 mL) can red kidney beans, drained and rinsed
1	(341 mL) can whole kernel corn, drained
	Salt and pepper
	Light sour cream
	Sliced green onion
	Grated cheddar cheese

In large heavy pot, heat oil over medium heat. Add beef, onion and garlic; saute for 7 minutes, breaking beef up with spoon and stirring frequently. Add bell pepper; saute for 5 minutes or until beef is no longer pink, and vegetables are tender. Drain off fat.

Add stock, stewed tomatoes, sun-dried tomatoes and bay leaves to beef mixture; increase heat to medium-high and bring to a boil. Reduce heat and simmer for 5 minutes. Add beans and corn; cook for 3 minutes or until heated through. Discard bay leaves. Add salt and pepper to taste. *(To freeze, see page 4.)* Top each serving with a dollop of sour cream, and a sprinkling of green onion and cheese.

Tip: Substitute 2 (540 mL) cans tomatoes for the 2 (540 mL) cans stewed tomatoes. Add 2 tablespoons (30 mL) chili powder and 1 teaspoon (5 mL) ground cumin just before adding bell pepper.

Makes 8 servings. PER SERVING: 238 cal, 20 g pro, 7 g fat, 26 g carb.

Goulash Soup

2	tablespoons (30 mL) all-purpose flour
1	tablespoon (15 mL) Hungarian sweet paprika
¼	teaspoon (1 mL) dried thyme leaves
	Salt and pepper
3	tablespoons (45 mL) extra-virgin olive oil, divided
1½	pounds (750 g) inside round beef steak (½-inch/1 cm thick), cut into ½-inch (1 cm) cubes
1	large onion, chopped
3	garlic cloves, minced
4	cups (1 L) beef stock
2	tablespoons (30 mL) tomato paste
1	bay leaf
1	(398 mL) can diced tomatoes, drained
1	red bell pepper, chopped coarse
1	teaspoon (5 mL) fresh lemon juice
4	cups (1 L) medium egg noodles
	Light sour cream
	Chopped fresh Italian (flat-leaf) parsley

In small bowl, combine flour, paprika, thyme, ¾ teaspoon (4 mL) salt and ¼ teaspoon (1 mL) pepper.

In large heavy pot, heat 2 tablespoons (30 mL) oil over medium-high heat. Add beef, in batches, and saute for 4 minutes or until browned. Using slotted spoon, transfer beef to heatproof bowl. Drain drippings from pot into bowl of beef; set aside.

Reduce heat to medium-low and add remaining 1 tablespoon (15 mL) oil to pot. Add onion and garlic; saute for 8 minutes or until tender.

Sprinkle onion mixture with flour mixture; cook for 1 minute, stirring constantly. Gradually stir in stock. Add 2 cups (500 mL) water, tomato paste and bay leaf. Add beef and drippings; increase heat to medium-high and bring to a boil, stirring occasionally. Reduce heat and simmer, covered, for 1 hour or until beef is tender. Add drained tomatoes and bell pepper; simmer, covered, for 5 minutes or until pepper is tender. Discard bay leaf. Add lemon juice. *(To freeze, see page 4.)*

Cook noodles in large pot of boiling salted water for 5 to 6 minutes or until tender; drain.

Divide noodles among 8 bowls. Add an equal portion of hot soup to each bowl. Top each serving with a dollop of sour cream and a sprinkling of parsley.

Tips

• *Paprika varies in flavour from mild to pungent and hot. Hungarian sweet paprika is a powder made by grinding sweet red peppers and has a mild flavour. We prefer Hungarian sweet paprika in this recipe but If you can't locate it, just substitute regular (not hot) paprika found in supermarkets.*

• *You can drink the juice that is drained from the can of diced tomatoes or use in another dish.*

Makes 8 servings. PER SERVING: 282 cal, 27 g pro, 9 g fat, 23 g carb.

Moroccan Lamb Soup with Harissa

1	tablespoon (15 mL) extra-virgin olive oil
1	pound (500 g) ground lamb
1	onion, chopped
4	garlic cloves, minced
1	teaspoon (5 mL) Hungarian sweet paprika
¼	cup (50 mL) Moroccan harissa (see tip)
1	(398 mL) can diced tomatoes
	Pinch saffron threads, crushed
½	cup (125 mL) broken vermicelli
1	(540 mL) can chickpeas, drained and rinsed
½	cup (125 mL) chopped fresh Italian (flat-leaf) parsley
½	cup (125 mL) chopped fresh cilantro
	Salt and pepper

In large heavy pot, heat oil over medium heat. Add lamb, onion and garlic; saute for 7 to 8 minutes or until onion is tender. Drain off fat.

Add paprika and harissa to lamb mixture; cook for 1 minute, stirring constantly. Add 5 cups (1.25 mL) water and tomatoes; increase heat to high and bring to a boil. Add saffron. Add vermicelli; reduce heat and boil gently for 7 minutes or until pasta is almost tender. Add chickpeas; cook for 2 minutes or until pasta is tender. Add parsley and cilantro. Add salt and pepper to taste. *(To freeze, see page 4.)*

Tips

• Harissa is a fiery chili paste. Different brands vary in heat intensity depending on the variety of chili and other ingredients used. In this recipe, be sure to use the jar labelled Moroccan harissa — containing hot pepper, bell pepper, preserved lemon, tomato, garlic, spices, oil and salt — not the tubes of harissa paste, as the flavour is too hot. Look for it in specialty food shops.

• Saffron threads don't lose their flavour as quickly as powdered saffron.

Makes 8 servings. PER SERVING: 287 cal, 15 g pro, 13 g fat, 26 g carb.

Old-Fashioned Ham Soup

1   leftover ham bone (with a small amount of ham still attached to bone)
1   large onion, chopped
2   bay leaves
2⅓   cups (575 mL) soup mix (a dry mix of yellow and green split peas, red lentils, alphabet pasta, pot barley and rice)
1½   teaspoons (7 mL) dried Italian seasoning
6   large carrots, sliced
2   celery stalks, sliced
        Salt and pepper

Put ham bone, onion and bay leaves in large heavy pot. Add 16 cups (4 L) water. (The ham bone should be completely covered. If necessary, add a little more water.) Place over high heat and bring to a boil. Reduce heat and simmer, covered, for 4 hours. Remove from stove and uncover; let cool slightly, then set pot in sink containing enough cold water to reach halfway up side of pot; stir frequently to cool stock quickly. Cover and refrigerate stock overnight.

Next day, remove fat from surface of ham stock; discard fat. Remove ham bone; set aside. Place pot of stock over high heat and bring to a boil. Meanwhile, cut ham from bone; discard bone. Cut ham into bite-size pieces (about 2 cups/500 mL); refrigerate until ready to add to soup.

When stock comes to a boil, add soup mix and Italian seasoning. Return to a boil; reduce heat and simmer, covered, for 50 minutes, stirring occasionally. Add carrots and celery. Increase heat and bring to a boil. Reduce heat and simmer for 15 minutes or until carrots and soup mix are tender, stirring occasionally. Add ham; cook for 2 minutes. Discard bay leaves. Add salt and pepper to taste. *(To freeze, see page 4.)*

Tip: A 250-gram bag of soup mix yields 2½ cups (625 mL).

Makes 12 servings. PER SERVING: 190 cal, 12 g pro, 2 g fat, 33 g carb.

Yellow Split Pea Soup

1	leftover ham bone (with a small amount of ham still attached to bone)
1	onion studded with 4 whole cloves
2	bay leaves
1	teaspoon (5 mL) dry mustard
2	cups (500 mL) yellow split peas, picked clean of debris and rinsed
1	teaspoon (5 mL) dried thyme leaves
3	large carrots, diced
2	celery stalks, diced
1	large leek, sliced thin
1	tablespoon (15 mL) red wine vinegar
	Salt and pepper
	Chopped fresh Italian (flat-leaf) parsley

Put ham bone, clove-studded onion and bay leaves in large heavy pot. Add 16 cups (4 L) water. (The ham bone should be completely covered. If necessary, add a little more water.) Place over high heat and bring to a boil. Reduce heat and simmer, covered, for 4 hours. Remove from stove and uncover; let cool slightly, then set pot in sink containing enough cold water to reach halfway up side of pot; stir frequently to cool stock quickly. Cover and refrigerate stock overnight.

Next day, remove fat from surface of ham stock; discard fat. Remove clove-studded onion and discard. Remove ham bone; set aside.

Transfer 1 tablespoon (15 mL) cold ham stock to small bowl. Add mustard and stir until dissolved. Add split peas, thyme and mustard mixture to ham stock. Place over high heat and bring to a boil.

Meanwhile, cut ham from bone; discard bone. Cut ham into bite-size pieces (about 2 cups/500 mL); refrigerate until ready to add to soup.

When stock comes to a boil, add carrots, celery and leek. Return to a boil; reduce heat and simmer, uncovered, for 75 minutes or until peas disintegrate and thicken soup, stirring occasionally then more frequently as soup thickens.

Add ham to soup; cook for 2 minutes. Discard bay leaves. Add vinegar. Add salt and pepper to taste. *(To freeze, see page 4.)* Top each serving with a sprinkling of parsley.

Tips

• *After any feast that includes baked ham, be sure to keep the leftover ham bone with a small amount of ham still attached to it — it can be transformed into this hearty soup for supper with enough left to stash in the freezer.*

• *To clean a leek, remove any withered outer leaves. Cut off and discard the green upper leaves down to the point where the dark green begins to pale. Trim off the root without disturbing the base. Halve lengthwise to within 1½-inches (4 cm) of the base, keeping the stalk intact. Rinse under cold running water to remove any grit trapped between the leaf layers. Slice leek, discarding base end.*

• *The trick to making the rich creamy texture typical of this classic soup is to cook the split peas until they disintegrate and thicken the stock.*

Makes 8 servings. PER SERVING: 262 cal, 21 g pro, 3 g fat, 40 g carb.

Black Bean Soup
with Italian Sausage and Spinach

1	tablespoon (15 mL) extra-virgin olive oil
¾	pound (350 g) hot Italian sausages, cut into ½-inch (1 cm) pieces
1	small onion, chopped
2	garlic cloves, minced
1½	cups (375 mL) chicken stock
1	(540 mL) can tomatoes (undrained), chopped coarse
1	(398 mL) can black beans, drained and rinsed
2	tablespoons (30 mL) chopped, drained sun-dried tomatoes (oil-packed)
1	tablespoon (15 mL) chopped fresh oregano
1	teaspoon (5 mL) chopped fresh thyme
12	cups (3 L) lightly packed fresh spinach (1 bunch), chopped coarse
	Salt and pepper

In large heavy pot, heat oil over medium-high heat. Add sausages; saute for 5 minutes or until cooked. Transfer sausages to heatproof bowl. Drain off all but 1 tablespoon (15 mL) fat from pot.

Add onion and garlic to pot; saute for 3 minutes or until tender. Add stock, tomatoes, beans, sun-dried tomatoes, oregano, thyme and sausages; bring to a boil. Add spinach; cook until spinach wilts. Add salt and pepper to taste. *(To freeze, see page 4.)*

Tips
• Use scissors to chop canned tomatoes right in the can. You'll save a little time and a lot of cleanup.
• For convenience, purchase washed, ready-to-use spinach:
A 283-gram package yields about 12 cups (3 L) lightly packed.
• Different brands of sun-dried tomatoes vary in flavour, so experiment until you find one you like.

Makes 4 servings. PER SERVING: 424 cal, 24 g pro, 24 g fat, 28 g carb.

Tortellini Soup with Spinach

1	tablespoon (15 mL) extra-virgin olive oil
2	ounces (60 g) thinly sliced prosciutto, chopped coarse
1	large onion, chopped
3	garlic cloves, minced
1	(350 g) package fresh cheese tortellini
8	cups (2 L) chicken stock
1	(540 mL) can white kidney or cannellini beans, drained and rinsed
4	cups (1 L) lightly packed fresh baby spinach
1	tablespoon (15 mL) fresh lemon juice
½	cup (125 mL) chopped fresh Italian (flat-leaf) parsley
¼	cup (50 mL) chopped fresh basil
	Salt and pepper
	Grated parmesan cheese

Put large pot of salted water over high heat and bring to a boil (for cooking tortellini).

Meanwhile, in large heavy pot, heat oil over medium-low heat. Add prosciutto; saute for 3 to 5 minutes or until crisp. With slotted spoon, remove prosciutto; set aside. Add onion and garlic to pot; increase heat to medium and saute for 4 minutes or until tender. (Now is the time to add tortellini to pot of boiling water and boil gently for 8 minutes or until tender.) Add stock to onion mixture; increase heat to medium-high, cover and bring to a simmer.

Drain cooked tortellini and add along with beans and spinach to stock mixture; cook until spinach wilts. Add lemon juice, parsley and basil. Add salt and pepper to taste. Top each serving with some of the prosciutto and a sprinkling of parmesan cheese.

Tip: *Nothing else quite delivers the intense, distinct flavour like salt-cured, air-dried prosciutto (Italian ham).*

Makes 8 servings. PER SERVING: 229 cal, 17 g pro, 7 g fat, 25 g carb.

Cabbage and Sweet Sausage Soup

1	tablespoon (15 mL) extra-virgin olive oil
1	pound (500 g) sweet Italian sausages, casings removed
1	large onion, chopped
3	garlic cloves, minced
¼	teaspoon (1 mL) dried crushed hot red pepper
6	cups (1.5 L) chicken stock
4	cups (1 L) shredded cabbage
2	cups (500 mL) grated carrots
1	(540 mL) can mixed beans, drained and rinsed
½	cup (125 mL) chopped fresh Italian (flat-leaf) parsley
	Salt and pepper

In large heavy pot, heat oil over medium heat. Add sausage, onion and garlic; saute for 12 minutes or until sausage is cooked and onion is tender, breaking up sausage with spoon and stirring frequently. Add dried red pepper. Drain off fat.

Add stock to sausage mixture; increase heat to high, cover and bring to a boil. Add cabbage and carrots; bring to a boil, uncovered. Reduce heat and boil gently for 5 minutes or until cabbage and carrots are just tender. Add beans; heat through. Add parsley. Add salt and pepper to taste. *(To freeze, see page 4.)*

Tips

• *For convenience, purchase bags of washed and ready-to-eat coleslaw (an undressed mixture of shredded cabbage and carrot) and washed and ready-to-eat shredded carrots.*
• *You can substitute your favourite bean for the mixed beans. To replace 1 (540 mL) can mixed beans, you'll need about 2 cups (500 mL) of cooked beans.*
• *We used sweet Italian sausages seasoned with sweet basil.*

Makes 8 servings. PER SERVING: 315 cal, 18 g pro, 17 g fat, 22 g carb.

Soba Noodle Soup with Edamame

2	tablespoons (30 mL) extra-virgin olive oil, divided
2	garlic cloves, minced
1	tablespoon (15 mL) minced fresh ginger
⅛	teaspoon (0.5 mL) dried crushed hot red pepper
¼	pound (125 g) snow peas, trimmed and halved
4	cups (1 L) chicken stock
2	teaspoons (10 mL) mirin (Japanese rice wine)
1	cup (250 mL) frozen shelled edamame (green soy beans)
½	pound (250 g) soba noodles (made from a combination of buckwheat and wheat flours)
½	pound (250 g) medium-firm tofu, cut into ½-inch (1 cm) cubes
2	teaspoons (10 mL) toasted sesame oil
1	green onion, sliced
	Toasted sesame seeds

Put large pot of salted water over high heat and bring to a boil (for cooking noodles). Meanwhile, in large heavy pot, heat 1 tablespoon (15 mL) olive oil over medium heat. Add garlic, ginger and dried red pepper; saute for 30 seconds. Add remaining 1 tablespoon (15 mL) olive oil. Add snow peas; saute for 1 minute. Add stock and mirin; increase heat to medium-high and bring to a boil. Add edamame. (Now is the time to add noodles to pot of boiling water and cook according to package directions.) Cook soup for 3 minutes. Add tofu; reduce heat and simmer for 2 minutes or until edamame is just tender.

Drain cooked noodles and return to their pot. Immediately add sesame oil to noodles; toss. Put an equal portion of noodles and soup into each of 4 bowls. Top each serving with a sprinkling of green onion and sesame seeds.

Tip: *Toasted sesame oil with its intense nutty flavour is made from sesame seeds that are toasted before extracting the oil.*

Makes 4 servings. PER SERVING: 469 cal, 26 g pro, 17 g fat, 55 g carb.

Lentil and Kale Soup

2	tablespoons (30 mL) extra-virgin olive oil
¼	pound (125 g) thinly sliced prosciutto, chopped coarse
2	onions, chopped
4	garlic cloves, minced
⅛	teaspoon (0.5 mL) dried crushed hot red pepper
4	carrots, diced
8	cups (2 L) coarsely chopped, stemmed kale
12	cups (3 L) chicken stock
2	(540 mL) cans lentils, drained and rinsed
2	tablespoons (30 mL) fresh lemon juice
1	cup (250 mL) chopped fresh Italian (flat-leaf) parsley
	Salt and pepper

In large heavy pot, heat oil over medium heat. Add prosciutto; saute for 3 minutes. Add onions, garlic and dried red pepper; saute for 3 minutes. Add carrots and kale; saute for 2 minutes. Add stock and lentils; increase heat to high and bring to a boil. Reduce heat and simmer, partially covered, for 10 minutes or until vegetables are tender. Set aside and let cool slightly.

Remove 7 cups (1.75 L) of soup and process in blender, in batches, until smooth. Transfer pureed soup back to pot; heat through. Add lemon juice and parsley. Add salt and pepper to taste. *(To freeze, see page 4.)*

Tips
• If desired, substitute 6 coarsely chopped bacon slices for the prosciutto. Or, omit prosciutto/bacon and add ¼ pound (125 g) diced smoked turkey at end of simmering time and heat through.
• Flat-leaf parsley has a fresh, peppery taste and is stronger in flavour than curly parsley. Wash parsley, shake off excess moisture, and wrap in paper towels. Store in a plastic bag; refrigerate for up to 1 week.
• If you cook your own lentils, you'll need 4 cups (1 L) cooked lentils.

Makes 8 servings. PER SERVING: 201 cal, 13 g pro, 5 g fat, 29 g carb.

Super-Fast Lentil Soup

1   tablespoon (15 mL) extra-virgin olive oil
½   cup (125 mL) thinly sliced carrots
1   onion, chopped
2   large garlic cloves, minced
1   tablespoon (15 mL) sun-dried tomato pesto
4   cups (1 L) vegetable stock
1   cup (250 mL) small cauliflowerets
¼   teaspoon (1 mL) dried thyme leaves
4   cups (1 L) lightly packed fresh spinach, chopped coarse
1   (540 mL) can lentils, drained and rinsed
1   tablespoon (15 mL) fresh lemon juice
     Salt and pepper

In large heavy pot, heat oil over medium-high heat. Add carrots, onion and garlic; saute for 3 minutes or until onion is tender. Remove from heat; add pesto and stir until well mixed with vegetables. Add stock, cauliflowerets and thyme. Place over high heat and bring to a boil. Reduce heat and simmer for 3 minutes or until cauliflowerets and carrots are almost tender. Add spinach and lentils; cook until spinach wilts. Add lemon juice. Add salt and pepper to taste. *(To freeze, see page 4.)*

Tip: *Keep packaged ready-to-use fresh vegetables (for this recipe you'll need cauliflower and spinach), sun-dried tomato pesto (refrigerated or bottled), canned lentils and dried thyme on hand. If spinach isn't a favourite, leave it out and increase the carrots and cauliflower.*

Makes 4 servings. PER SERVING: 179 cal, 10 g pro, 6 g fat, 25 g carb.

I'm-Too-Busy-To-Cook Bean Soup

6	cups (1.5 L) vegetable stock
2	(398 mL) cans stewed tomatoes
2	(398 mL) cans navy beans, drained and rinsed
3	cups (750 mL) frozen mixed vegetables
	Dash hot pepper sauce
½	cup (125 mL) chopped fresh Italian (flat-leaf) parsley
	Salt and pepper
	Grated parmesan cheese

In large heavy pot, combine stock, stewed tomatoes and beans. Place over high heat and bring to a boil. Add frozen vegetables and return to a boil; reduce heat and simmer for 2 minutes. Add hot pepper sauce and parsley. Add salt and pepper to taste. Top each serving with a sprinkling of parmesan cheese.

Tips

• The beauty of this incredibly easy soup is that it doesn't require any sauteing. Simply combine all of the readily available ingredients in one big pot, and heat. Peer into your freezer and pull out any combination of mixed vegetables. We used a package that contained green beans, carrots, corn and peas.

• There is a variety of seasoned stewed tomatoes available nowadays. Select your favourite style of stewed tomatoes and omit the hot pepper sauce if desired.

• For optimum flavour, use fresh or frozen vegetable stock available at some markets; otherwise, reconstituted vegetable soup cubes will suffice. We found McCormick all-vegetable bouillon cubes, dissolved in water according to package directions, to be a good substitute.

Makes 6 servings. PER SERVING: 245 cal, 15 g pro, 3 g fat, 44 g carb.

Roasted Asparagus Soup

4   teaspoons (20 mL) extra-virgin olive oil
3   pounds (1.5 kg) asparagus, trimmed
1   tablespoon (15 mL) extra-virgin olive oil
1   large leek, sliced thin
1   garlic clove, minced
5   cups (1.25 L) chicken stock
1   Yukon Gold potato, cut into $\frac{1}{2}$-inch (1 cm) cubes
1   bay leaf
1   teaspoon (5 mL) fresh lemon juice
      Salt and pepper
      Light sour cream
$\frac{1}{2}$ cup (125 mL) shredded arugula

Drizzle 4 teaspoons (20 mL) oil over asparagus; toss. Place asparagus, in single layer, on 2 ungreased rimmed baking sheets. Roast at 500 F (260 C) for 5 to 8 minutes or until tender, turning asparagus once halfway through roasting time. Let asparagus cool slightly, then cut asparagus tips off; set 12 tips aside for garnish. Cut stalks into $\frac{1}{2}$-inch (1 cm) pieces; set aside.

In large heavy pot, heat 1 tablespoon (15 mL) oil over medium-low heat. Add leek; saute for 3 to 5 minutes or until tender. Add garlic; saute for 1 minute. Add stock, potato and bay leaf; increase heat to medium-high and bring to a boil. Reduce heat and simmer, covered, for 12 minutes or until potato is very tender. Add asparagus stalks and tips (except the tips set aside for garnish); simmer, uncovered, for 5 to 7 minutes or until stalks are very tender. Set aside and let cool slightly. Discard bay leaf.

In blender, process soup, in batches, until smooth; pour into large heatproof bowl. Transfer soup back to pot; heat through. Add lemon juice. Add salt and pepper to taste.

Cut the 12 asparagus tips in half lengthwise. Top each serving with a dollop of sour cream, and a sprinkling of asparagus tips and arugula.

Makes 6 servings. PER SERVING: 141 cal, 10 g pro, 6 g fat, 16 g carb.

48

Creamy Beet Soup

8	beets (2 pounds/1 kg total)
2	tablespoons (30 mL) extra-virgin olive oil
	Salt and pepper
2	large carrots, cut in half lengthwise, then crosswise into 1-inch (2.5 cm) pieces
2	onions, each cut into 8 wedges
3	large garlic cloves
3	cups (750 mL) chicken stock
½	cup (125 mL) dry red wine
1	tablespoon (15 mL) fresh lemon juice
1	teaspoon (5 mL) prepared horseradish
1	tablespoon (15 mL) chopped fresh dill
	Light sour cream, optional
	Chopped fresh chives or dill

Peel beets; cut each beet into 8 wedges. In large bowl, whisk together oil, 1 teaspoon (5 mL) salt and ¼ teaspoon (1 mL) pepper; add beets, carrots, onions and garlic cloves and toss. Place vegetables, in single layer, in 2 (13x9-inch/33x23 cm) ungreased baking dishes; cover tightly with foil. Bake at 375 F (190 C) for 70 minutes or until beets are tender. Uncover; turn vegetables over. Bake, uncovered, for 10 minutes.

Meanwhile, in large heavy saucepan, combine stock, 1¾ cups (425 mL) water and wine. Place over high heat and bring to a boil; boil for 10 to 12 minutes or until liquid is reduced to 4 cups (1 L). Add lemon juice and horseradish. Set aside and let cool slightly.

In blender, process vegetables and any accumulated liquid, and stock mixture, in batches, until smooth; transfer soup to large heavy pot. Add ½ cup (125 mL) water; heat through. Add 1 tablespoon (15 mL) dill. Add salt and pepper to taste. *(To freeze, see page 4.)* Top each serving with a dollop of sour cream and a sprinkling of chives.

Makes 6 servings. PER SERVING: 174 cal, 6 g pro, 6 g fat, 23 g carb.

Cheddar Broccoli Soup

¾   pound (350 g) broccoli, trimmed
2   tablespoons (30 mL) all-purpose flour
¼   teaspoon (1 mL) dry mustard
¼   teaspoon (1 mL) Hungarian sweet paprika
1   tablespoon (15 mL) extra-virgin olive oil
1   carrot, diced
1   celery stalk, diced
1   onion, chopped
2   garlic cloves, minced
2   cups (500 mL) chicken stock
2   cups (500 mL) milk
2   cups (500 mL) grated medium cheddar cheese
     Salt and pepper
     Grated medium cheddar cheese

Bring large pot of water to a boil. Cut broccoli florets into tiny pieces; peel stalks and coarsely chop (4 cups/1 L total florets and stalks).

Add broccoli florets and stalks to boiling water; cook for 2 minutes or until tender-crisp. Drain and place broccoli in large amount of ice water until cool, about 3 minutes; drain well in sieve.

In small bowl, combine flour, mustard and paprika; set aside. In large heavy saucepan, heat oil over medium-low heat. Add carrot, celery, onion and garlic; cook for 10 to 12 minutes or until onion is tender, stirring frequently (do not brown). Reduce heat to low; sprinkle vegetables with flour mixture and cook for 2 minutes, stirring constantly. Gradually stir in stock, then milk; increase heat to medium-high and bring to a boil, stirring frequently. Reduce heat and simmer for 4 minutes, stirring frequently. Remove from heat; let stand for 3 minutes, stirring occasionally. Add 2 cups (500 mL) cheese, stirring until melted. Add broccoli. Place over low heat until broccoli is heated through (do not simmer). Add salt and pepper to taste. Top each serving with a sprinkling of cheese.

Makes 6 servings. PER SERVING: 305 cal, 19 g pro, 20 g fat, 13 g carb.

Spicy Thai Carrot and Coconut Soup

2	tablespoons (30 mL) extra-virgin olive oil, divided
	Salt and pepper
2	pounds (1 kg) large carrots, halved lengthwise and cut into 1-inch (2.5 cm) pieces (5 cups/1.25 L)
1	onion, chopped
3	garlic cloves, minced
2	tablespoons (30 mL) minced fresh ginger
2	lemon grass stalks, smashed and cut into 4-inch (10 cm) pieces
1	serrano pepper, seeded, deveined and chopped
6	cups (1.5 L) chicken stock
1	(398 mL) can regular (not light) coconut milk, stirred
2	tablespoons (30 mL) fresh lime juice
	Low-fat plain yogurt
	Coarsely chopped fresh cilantro

In large bowl, whisk together 1 tablespoon (15 mL) oil, and ¼ teaspoon (1 mL) each salt and pepper. Add carrots; toss. Place carrots, in single layer, on ungreased rimmed baking sheet. Roast at 375 F (190 C) for 55 minutes or until carrots are tender, stirring occasionally.

In large heavy pot, heat remaining 1 tablespoon (15 mL) oil over medium heat. Add onion, garlic, ginger, lemon grass and serrano pepper; saute for 5 minutes or until onion is tender. Add stock and roasted carrots; increase heat to high and bring to a boil. Reduce heat and simmer for 10 minutes. Set aside and let cool slightly. Discard lemon grass.

In blender, process soup, in batches, until smooth; pour into large heatproof bowl. Transfer soup back to pot. Add coconut milk and lime juice; place over medium-low heat and heat through (do not boil). Add salt and pepper to taste. *(To freeze, see page 4.)* Top each serving with a dollop of yogurt and a sprinkling of cilantro.

Tip: *To smash lemon grass, peel off tough outer leaves. Cover stalk with sheet of wax paper; smash with a meat cleaver.*

Makes 10 servings. PER SERVING: 178 cal, 6 g pro, 12 g fat, 14 g carb.

Roasted Cauliflower Soup

Soup

1	(2¼ pound/1 kg) cauliflower, trimmed
3	tablespoons (45 mL) extra-virgin olive oil, divided
	Salt and pepper
1	onion, chopped
2	garlic cloves, minced
⅓	cup (75 mL) dry white wine
7	cups (1.75 L) chicken stock
½	cup (125 mL) cream (10 per cent M.F.)

Topping

1	tablespoon (15 mL) extra-virgin olive oil
2	ounces (60 g) thinly sliced prosciutto, chopped
1	shallot, chopped fine
1	teaspoon (5 mL) butter, at room temperature
1	cup (250 mL) coarse fresh bread crumbs
¼	cup (50 mL) chopped fresh Italian (flat-leaf) parsley

Soup: Cut cauliflower into 2-inch (5 cm) florets (7 cups/1.75 L); pat dry. In large bowl, whisk together 2 tablespoons (30 mL) oil, ½ teaspoon (2 mL) salt and ¼ teaspoon (1 mL) pepper. Add florets; toss. Place florets, in single layer, on ungreased rimmed baking sheet. Roast at 475 F (240 C) for 18 to 20 minutes or until tender, turning florets once halfway through roasting time. Measure 1 cup (250 mL) roasted florets; remove stems and reserve. Cut stemmed florets into tiny florets; reserve for garnish.

In large heavy pot, heat remaining 1 tablespoon (15 mL) oil over medium heat. Add onion and garlic; saute for 3 to 5 minutes or until onion is tender. Add wine; cook for 1 to 2 minutes or until liquid is mostly evaporated, stirring frequently. Add stock, roasted cauliflower and reserved cauliflower stems; increase heat to high and bring to a boil. Reduce heat and simmer for 25 minutes or until cauliflower is very tender, stirring occasionally. Set aside and let cool slightly.

In blender, process soup, in batches, until smooth; pour into large heatproof bowl. Transfer soup back to pot. Add cream; place over medium-low heat and heat through (do not boil). Add salt and pepper to taste. *(To freeze, see page 4.)*

Topping: In medium-size heavy frypan, heat oil over medium-low heat. Add prosciutto; saute for 3 minutes or until beginning to crisp. Add shallot; saute for 1 to 2 minutes or until prosciutto is crisp. Add butter; stir until melted. Add bread crumbs; saute for 2 minutes. Add parsley. Top each serving of soup with a sprinkling of topping and reserved tiny florets.

Tips

• For best results, use a rimmed baking sheet that is a regular shiny sheet. We roasted cauliflower on a dark, non-stick baking sheet and in a baking dish, and found the cauliflower browned more evenly on a regular shiny baking sheet.

• To make soft, coarse bread crumbs, tear bread in pieces and process in food processor.

• Prepare bread crumb topping while soup is simmering.

• Parmesan Cheese and Parsley Topping variation: Omit bread crumb topping. Top each serving of soup with a sprinkling of parmesan cheese and chopped fresh Italian (flat-leaf) parsley.

Makes 8 servings. PER SERVING: 231 cal, 11 g pro, 11 g fat, 20 g carb.

Creamy Woodland Mushroom Soup

Soup

2	tablespoons (30 mL) extra-virgin olive oil
2	tablespoons (30 mL) butter, at room temperature
4	shallots, chopped
3	garlic cloves, minced
2	pounds (1 kg) assorted mushrooms, sliced thick (mixture of cremini, oyster, portobello and shiitake)
¼	cup (50 mL) dry sherry
2	cups (500 mL) chicken stock
½	cup (125 mL) milk
½	cup (125 mL) whipping cream
1	teaspoon (5 mL) chopped fresh thyme
½	cup (125 mL) chopped fresh Italian (flat-leaf) parsley
	Salt and pepper

Topping

2	tablespoons (30 mL) extra-virgin olive oil
½	pound (250 g) assorted mushrooms, sliced
¼	cup (50 mL) whipping cream
½	cup (125 mL) low-fat plain yogurt

Soup: In large heavy pot, heat oil and butter over medium-low heat. Add shallots and garlic; saute for 5 minutes or until tender. Add thickly sliced mushrooms and increase heat to medium; saute for 15 minutes or until mushrooms release their liquid. Add sherry; cook for 2 minutes. Reduce heat and simmer, covered, for 25 minutes or until mushrooms are tender, stirring occasionally.

Add stock and 2 cups (500 mL) water to mushroom mixture; increase heat to medium-high, cover and bring to a boil. Reduce heat and simmer for 15 minutes. Set aside and let cool slightly.

In blender, process soup, in batches, until smooth; pour into large heatproof bowl. Transfer soup back to pot. Add milk, cream and thyme; place over medium-low heat and heat through (do not boil). Add parsley.

Add salt and pepper to taste. *(To freeze, see page 4.)*

Topping: In large heavy frypan, heat oil over medium-high heat. Add mushrooms and saute for 3 to 5 minutes or until tender. Meanwhile, beat whipping cream in small bowl until soft peaks form; fold in yogurt.

Top each serving of soup with a dollop of whipped cream mixture and an equal portion of sauteed mushrooms.

Tips

• Be sure to remove and discard the tough stems from shiitake mushrooms.

• Although among the most expensive of the onion clan, tender shallots are best known for their mild, sweet flavour. They resemble a large garlic bulb and can have two or three segmented cloves. One shallot refers to the whole bulb, not just one clove.

Makes 6 servings. PER SERVING: 306 cal, 9 g pro, 24 g fat, 15 g carb.

Onion and Cider Soup

Topping

16 (½-inch/1 cm) thick slices sourdough baguette
2 cups (500 mL) grated Oka cheese
½ cup (125 mL) grated parmesan cheese

Soup

¼ cup (50 mL) butter, at room temperature
3 large Spanish onions, sliced (2 pounds/1 kg total)
1 teaspoon (5 mL) granulated sugar
1 bay leaf
¼ cup (50 mL) all-purpose flour
8 cups (2 L) beef stock
2 cups (500 mL) sweet cider (fresh-pressed apple juice)
¼ cup (50 mL) port or dry sherry
2 teaspoons (10 mL) fresh thyme leaves
  Salt and pepper

Topping: Place baguette slices, in single layer, on ungreased rimmed baking sheet. Bake at 350 F (180 C) for 8 to 10 minutes or until dry, turning slices over once halfway through baking time. Let cool.

Soup: In large heavy pot, melt butter over medium-high heat. Add onions, sugar and bay leaf; saute for 10 minutes. Reduce heat to medium-low; cook for 25 minutes or until tender, stirring occasionally. Reduce heat to low; sprinkle onions with flour and cook for 2 minutes, stirring constantly. Gradually stir in stock, then cider, port and thyme; increase heat to high and bring to a boil, stirring occasionally. Reduce heat and simmer, covered, for 10 minutes, stirring occasionally. Discard bay leaf. Add salt and pepper to taste. *(To freeze, see page 4. Reheat before putting in bowls.)*

Set 8 ovenproof soup bowls on rimmed baking sheet. Divide soup among bowls. Top each with 2 toasted baguette slices; sprinkle with an equal portion of Oka and parmesan cheeses. Bake at 450 F (230 C) for 5 minutes or until cheese is melted and starting to brown.

Tips

• *The creamy, tangy somewhat pungent Oka cheese hails originally from Quebec. It has great melting properties and a nutty, fruity flavour — a suitable substitution is gruyere or Swiss cheese. You'll need about 6 ounces (170 g) Oka cheese to yield 2 cups (500 mL) grated cheese.*

• *We tested this recipe with both Spanish and regular yellow onions. We recommend seeking out Spanish onions — they're milder in flavour and when caramelized contribute an intense rich sweet flavour.*

• *Non-alcoholic or "sweet" cider is fresh-pressed apple juice (it's actually unsweetened); it becomes hard cider after fermentation, with a varying range of alcohol content.*

• *Beef stock adds a depth of flavour and richness but vegetable stock can be substituted.*

• *To slice onion, cut in half lengthwise. Lay onion half, cut side down, and slice crosswise into thin slices.*

Makes 8 servings. PER SERVING: 352 cal, 14 g pro, 15 g fat, 41 g carb.

Gingered Squash and Carrot Soup

1	(3-pound/1.5 kg) butternut squash
2	tablespoons (30 mL) extra-virgin olive oil
1	pound (500 g) carrots, cut into 1½-inch (4 cm) pieces (3 cups/750 mL)
2	onions, each cut into 6 wedges
5	garlic cloves (unpeeled)
6	cups (1.5 L) chicken stock
1½	teaspoons (7 mL) minced fresh ginger
¼	teaspoon (1 mL) grated nutmeg
¼	cup (50 mL) fresh orange juice
	Salt and pepper
	Light sour cream
	Chopped fresh Italian (flat-leaf) parsley

Cut butternut squash in half lengthwise; seed, peel and cut into 1½-inch (4 cm) pieces (9 cups/2.25 L).

Put oil in large bowl. Add squash, carrots and onions; toss. Place vegetables, in single layer, on ungreased rimmed baking sheet. Wrap unpeeled garlic cloves tightly in piece of foil; place on baking sheet with vegetables. Roast at 375 F (190 C) for 1 hour or until tender, turning vegetables once halfway through roasting time.

Squeeze garlic cloves out of their papery skins into small bowl.

In blender, process roasted vegetables and garlic, in batches, until smooth, adding enough stock to each batch to keep the blade from clogging; transfer soup to large heavy pot. Add remaining stock, ginger and nutmeg; bring to a simmer, stirring frequently. Add orange juice. Add salt and pepper to taste. *(To freeze, see page 4.)* Top each serving with a dollop of sour cream and a sprinkling of parsley.

Tip: For best flavour, use freshly grated whole nutmeg.

Makes 8 servings. PER SERVING: 164 cal, 3 g pro, 5 g fat, 31 g carb.

Mexican Pumpkin Soup

2	(2-pound/1 kg) pie or sugar pumpkins
	Extra-virgin olive oil
3	large carrots, sliced thin
2	large onions, sliced very thin
2	garlic cloves, minced
1	tablespoon (15 mL) finely chopped fresh ginger
1	jalapeno pepper, seeded and minced
2	teaspoons (10 mL) granulated sugar
7	cups (1.75 L) chicken stock
1	(540 mL) can red kidney beans, drained and rinsed
2	tablespoons (30 mL) fresh lime juice
	Salt and pepper
	Chopped fresh cilantro
	Tortilla chips, broken into pieces

Halve and seed pumpkins. Brush cut surfaces with oil; place, cut side down, in single layer, in ungreased baking dish. Bake at 375 F (190 C) for 1 hour or until very tender. Let cool; scrape out flesh and put in bowl.

In large heavy pot, heat 2 tablespoons (30 mL) oil over medium heat. Add carrots and onions; saute for 15 minutes or until onions are tender. Reduce heat to medium-low; add garlic, ginger and jalapeno pepper. Sprinkle with sugar; saute for 15 minutes or until onions are very tender. Add stock and pumpkin flesh; increase heat to medium-high and bring to a boil. Reduce heat and simmer for 5 minutes or until carrots are tender. Set aside and let cool slightly.

In blender, process soup, in batches, until smooth; pour into large heatproof bowl. Transfer soup back to pot. Add beans; heat through, stirring. Add lime juice. Add salt and pepper to taste. (*To freeze, see page 4.*) Top each serving with a sprinkling of cilantro and chips.

Tip: *Be sure to use the smaller pie pumpkins, as their flesh is sweeter and smoother than the large pumpkins used for Halloween jack-o'-lanterns.*

Makes 6 servings. PER SERVING: 318 cal, 13 g pro, 8 g fat, 53 g carb.

Roasted Tomato Soup

Croutons

1   cup (250 mL) cubed baguette
3   tablespoons (45 mL) butter, at room temperature
½   teaspoon (2 mL) dried crushed hot red pepper
1   tablespoon (15 mL) minced garlic
2   tablespoons (30 mL) finely chopped fresh Italian (flat-leaf) parsley
1   teaspoon (5 mL) dried herbes de provence (see tip)

Soup

2½   pounds (1.125 kg) plum tomatoes
     Extra-virgin olive oil
2   tablespoons (30 mL) dried herbes de provence (see tip)
     Salt and pepper
1   whole head garlic, separated into cloves and peeled
     Shredded fresh basil

Croutons: Put baguette cubes in small bowl. In small heavy saucepan, combine butter, dried red pepper, garlic, parsley and herbes de provence. Place over medium heat; cook for 3 minutes or until bubbles start to appear, stirring occasionally. Pour butter mixture over baguette cubes; mix well. Place, in single layer, on ungreased rimmed baking sheet. Bake at 400 F (200 C) for 8 minutes or until light golden. Remove from oven; transfer croutons to paper-towel-lined plate.

Soup: Cut tomatoes in half lengthwise; place, cut side up, on large ungreased rimmed baking sheet. Drizzle tomatoes with ⅓ cup (75 mL) oil. Sprinkle with herbes de provence, and ¼ teaspoon each (1 mL) salt and pepper. Roast at 400 F (200 C) for 1 hour or until tomatoes are soft and wrinkled.

In large heavy pot, combine tomatoes and their pan juices, 4 cups (1 L) water, garlic cloves and ¼ teaspoon (1 mL) salt; bring to a boil. Reduce heat and simmer for 30 minutes. Strain soup through fine sieve set over heatproof bowl, pressing on solids with wooden spoon. Add salt and pepper to taste. Top each serving with a sprinkling of basil and croutons, and a drizzle of oil.

Tips

• *Jean-Francis and Alessandra Quaglia, owners of Vancouver's Provence Mediterranean Grill and Provence Marinaside, shared this light but intensely flavourful soup with us. Herbes de provence is commonly used in southern France where the mixture often contains basil, fennel seed, lavender, marjoram, rosemary, sage, summer savory and thyme. The Quaglias recommend using herbes de provence that doesn't contain lavender. The dried herbs de provence used in this recipe was a blend of thyme, rosemary, bay leaf, basil and savory.*

• *To preserve flavour and texture, store tomatoes at room temperature.*

Makes 4 servings. PER SERVING: 410 cal, 6 g pro, 30 g fat, 33 g carb.

Roasted Vegetable Soup

1	fennel bulb, trimmed
3	tablespoons (45 mL) extra-virgin olive oil
	Salt and pepper
3	large carrots, halved lengthwise and cut into 1-inch (2.5 cm) pieces
1	red onion, cut into ¼-inch (5 mm) thick slices
4	large garlic cloves, smashed
1	large red bell pepper, cut into quarters
2	cups (500 mL) cubed (1½-inch/4 cm) peeled butternut squash
8	cups (2 L) chicken or vegetable stock
1	teaspoon (5 mL) fresh lemon juice
½	cup (125 mL) chopped fresh Italian (flat-leaf) parsley
2	cups (500 mL) Rosemary Croutons (see recipe, page 87)

Cut fennel in half lengthwise and remove core. Place each half, cut side down, and cut lengthwise into ¼-inch (5 mm) thick slices; cut each slice in half, lengthwise.

In large bowl, whisk together oil, 1 teaspoon (5 mL) salt and ¼ teaspoon (1 mL) pepper. Add fennel, carrots, onion, garlic, bell pepper and squash to oil mixture; toss. Place vegetables, in single layer, in 2 parchment-paper-lined rimmed baking sheets. Roast at 375 F (190 C) for 50 to 60 minutes or until vegetables are tender and starting to brown, turning once halfway through roasting time. Remove and discard skin from peppers.

In blender, process roasted vegetables and stock, in batches, until smooth; transfer soup to large heavy pot and heat through. *(To freeze, see page 4.)* Add lemon juice and parsley. Add salt and pepper to taste. Top each serving with croutons.

Tip: *For best results, smash garlic cloves with the flat side of chef's knife, rather than crushing them in a press.*

Makes 8 servings. PER SERVING: 175 cal, 7 g pro, 9 g fat, 17 g carb.

Watercress Soup

2	tablespoons (30 mL) extra-virgin olive oil
1	large onion, chopped
1	potato, diced
	Salt and pepper
2½	cups (625 mL) chicken or vegetable stock
2½	cups (625 mL) homogenized milk
3	bunches watercress (about 1½ pounds/750 g), thick stalks removed
¼	cup (50 mL) whipping cream, whipped
	Watercress sprigs

In large heavy pot, heat oil over medium heat. Add onion and potato; stir until vegetables are well coated. Sprinkle lightly with salt and pepper. Reduce heat to low; cook, covered, for 12 minutes or until onion is tender, stirring occasionally.

Add stock and milk; increase heat to medium and bring to a simmer. Reduce heat and simmer, covered, for 10 minutes or until potato is tender (do not boil). Add 3 bunches watercress and simmer, uncovered, for 4 to 5 minutes or until watercress is just tender. Set aside and let cool slightly.

In blender, process soup, in batches, until smooth; pour into large heatproof bowl. *(To freeze, see page 4.)* Transfer soup back to pot and place over medium-low heat until heated through (do not boil). Add salt and pepper to taste. Top each serving with a dollop of whipped cream and a watercress sprig.

Tip: *After returning from culinary study in Ballymaloe, Ireland, Adrienne O'Callaghan prepared this soup in* The Vancouver Sun *Test Kitchen. Her soup was an instant five-star hit. Adrienne O'Callaghan was a resident chef and instructor at Barbara-Jo's Books to Cooks in Vancouver before taking a recent hiatus from her career to raise her twin daughters.*

Makes 6 servings. PER SERVING: 166 cal, 9 g pro, 9 g fat, 13 g carb.

Chilled Strawberry Dessert Soup (recipe on following page)

Cold Soups

Chilled Strawberry Dessert Soup

1	cup (250 mL) granulated sugar
1	vanilla bean
1	cup (250 mL) Moscato wine (see tip)
1	lemon
6	cups (1.5 L) sliced strawberries
½	cup (125 mL) whipping cream, whipped
	Dark chocolate curls

Put sugar in small heavy saucepan. Cut vanilla bean in half lengthwise and scrape seeds into sugar; whisk to disperse seeds. Cut vanilla bean halves, crosswise, in half; add to sugar. Add 1 cup (250 mL) water and wine.

Using vegetable peeler, remove zest, in strips, from lemon. Add zest to wine mixture. Place over high heat and bring to a boil, stirring constantly until sugar dissolves. Reduce heat and simmer for 5 minutes. Let syrup cool completely. Cover tightly and refrigerate overnight or until well chilled. Discard vanilla bean pieces and lemon zest.

In blender, process strawberries with syrup, in batches, until smooth; pour into large bowl. Cover and refrigerate overnight or until well chilled. *(To freeze, see page 4.)* Whisk soup, then divide among 12 chilled dessert dishes. Top each serving with a dollop of whipped cream and a sprinkling of chocolate curls.

Tips

• *Raspberry variation: Substitute whole raspberries for sliced strawberries. Put pureed raspberry soup in fine sieve to remove seeds.*
• *Moscato wine is an Italian wine made from the muscat grape variety. For this recipe, we chose a white wine called Moscato Delle Venezie with slightly sweet, gently fizzy characteristics.*
• *If you prefer a slightly sweeter soup, add 1 tablespoon (15 mL) granulated sugar to whipping cream before whipping.*
• *Leftover soup makes a luscious topping for ice cream.*

Makes 12 servings. PER SERVING: 163 cal, 1 g pro, 4 g fat, 27 g carb.

Gazpacho

1¾	pounds (850 g) tomatoes, peeled, seeded and chopped coarse
½	cup (125 mL) each coarsely chopped red and yellow bell pepper
1	English cucumber, peeled and chopped coarse
1	small sweet onion, chopped coarse
2	garlic cloves, chopped
¼	cup (50 mL) extra-virgin olive oil
2	tablespoons (30 mL) white balsamic vinegar
½	teaspoon (2 mL) roasted cumin seeds, ground
1½	cups (375 mL) vegetable cocktail
	Salt and pepper
	Rosemary Croutons (see recipe, page 87), optional

In large bowl, combine tomatoes, bell peppers, cucumber, onion, garlic, oil, vinegar, cumin and vegetable cocktail. In blender, process tomato mixture, in batches, until smooth; transfer to large bowl. Add salt and pepper to taste. Cover and refrigerate overnight or until well chilled. Whisk soup, before serving. Top each serving with croutons.

Tips

• *To roast cumin seeds, place in small heavy frypan over medium-high heat; cook for 1 to 2 minutes or until fragrant, stirring constantly. Let seeds cool, then grind in spice mill or mortar and pestle.*

• *For exquisite flavour, be sure to use ripe juicy field tomatoes.*

• *To peel tomatoes, bring large pot of water to a boil. Add tomatoes and blanch for about 30 seconds. Drain tomatoes, rinse with cold water, then peel.*

• *To seed tomato, cut in half horizontally, then use a spoon to remove seeds and pulp.*

• *Sweet onions are milder and juicier than regular onions. Their high moisture content also makes them more perishable than other onions, so store them in the refrigerator and don't keep them too long. Sweet varieties include Maui, Vidalia, Walla Walla, Texas Sweets and Mayan.*

Makes 6 servings. PER SERVING: 135 cal, 2 g pro, 8 g fat, 16 g carb.

Soupe Aux Fruits Rouges

1½   cups (375 mL) granulated sugar
2½   cups (625 mL) fresh or frozen raspberries, thawed
1   tablespoon (15 mL) fresh lemon juice
6   cups (1.5 L) mixed fruit (any combination of blackberries, blueberries, halved and pitted cherries, red currants, raspberries, and quartered strawberries)
      Fresh lemon balm or mint sprigs

In medium-size heavy saucepan, combine sugar and 1¼ cups (300 mL) water. Place over medium-low heat; cook until sugar dissolves, stirring constantly. Increase heat and bring to a boil; boil for 1 minute. Remove from heat; let syrup cool completely.

In food processor, process 2½ cups (625 mL) raspberries, cooled sugar syrup and lemon juice until smooth. Strain raspberry mixture through fine sieve set over large bowl; set sauce aside.

Spoon some of the mixed fruit into glass bowl or among 4 dessert glasses. Ladle some of the raspberry sauce on top. Continue to layer fruit with sauce until all of the ingredients are used. Top each serving with a lemon balm sprig.

Tips

• *This eye-catching chilled fruit soup recipe was brought into our kitchen by Suzanne Quaglia, a highly regarded chef visiting from Marseilles, France. Her son and daughter-in-law, Jean-Francis and Alessandra, own the Provence Mediterranean Grill and Provence Marinaside restaurants in Vancouver.*

• *The raspberry sauce is particularly useful as it can be made at any time of the year and used to top fresh fruit and as a companion for canned peaches or pears, cake or ice cream.*

Makes 4 servings. PER SERVING: 438 cal, 2 g pro, 1 g fat, 111 g carb.

Chilled Ginger Peach Soup

7	cups (1.75 L) sliced peeled peaches (14 medium)
½	cup (125 mL) sweet white wine
¼	cup (50 mL) granulated sugar
1	tablespoon (15 mL) fresh lemon juice
½	cup (125 mL) french vanilla yogurt (3.2 per cent M.F.)
	Preserved ginger syrup (see tip)
	Fresh mint leaves

Coarsely chop and put peaches in large heavy pot. Add wine, sugar and lemon juice. Place over medium heat and bring to a simmer, stirring occasionally; simmer for 2 minutes. Set aside and let cool slightly.

In blender, process peach mixture, in batches, until smooth; pour into large heatproof bowl. Refrigerate until well chilled, stirring occasionally.

Whisk yogurt into chilled peach mixture. *(To freeze, see page 4.)* Cover and refrigerate for up to 1 day. Whisk soup, then divide soup among 8 chilled dessert dishes. Top each serving with a drizzle of ginger syrup and a mint sprig.

Tips

• *Preserved ginger is similar to crystallized ginger but instead of being coated with sugar, the translucent pieces of ginger are packed in a jar with syrup. Both the ginger and syrup can be used to flavour sweet and savoury dishes.*

• *Cold soups are best served in chilled dessert dishes. To chill dishes, put them in the refrigerator for 30 minutes before ladling soup into them.*

• *If there's any peach soup left over, it's wonderful drizzled over your favourite vanilla or peach ice cream.*

• *To peel peaches easily, bring large pot of water to a boil. Add peaches and blanch for 30 seconds. Drain peaches then submerge in cold water to cool; remove and peel.*

Makes 8 servings. PER SERVING: 121 cal, 2 g pro, 1 g fat, 27 g carb.

Chilled Garlic and Sorrel Soup

4	whole heads garlic (7 ounces/200 g total)
¼	cup (50 mL) butter, at room temperature
1	large onion, chopped
2	large potatoes, cubed
1	teaspoon (5 mL) salt
½	teaspoon (2 mL) white pepper
3	fresh thyme sprigs
1	bay leaf
¾	cup (175 mL) cream (10 per cent M.F.)
	Creme fraiche or light sour cream
	Shredded sorrel leaves

Separate garlic heads into cloves and peel. In medium-size heavy saucepan, bring enough water to cover garlic to a boil. Add garlic cloves; boil for 2 minutes. Strain; discard water. Repeat process two more times.

In large heavy saucepan, heat butter over medium-high heat. Add onion; saute for 3 minutes or until tender but not brown. Add boiled garlic cloves; saute for 30 seconds. Add 4 cups (1 L) water, potatoes, salt, pepper, thyme and bay leaf; bring to a boil. Reduce heat and simmer for 40 minutes, stirring occasionally. Discard thyme sprigs and bay leaf. Set aside and let cool slightly.

In blender, process soup, in batches, until smooth. Strain soup through fine sieve set over large heatproof bowl. Let cool slightly, then cover and refrigerate overnight or until well chilled. Stir cream into soup. Top each serving with a dollop of creme fraiche and a sprinkling of sorrel.

Tips

• *Vancouver chef Dino Gazzola made this divine summer soup in 1995 — it's still requested by our readers.*

• *Creme fraiche is slightly thickened cream that has a tangy flavour and velvety rich texture.*

Makes 4 servings. PER SERVING: 215 cal, 4 g pro, 16 g fat, 16 g carb.

Pita Crisps with Moroccan Seasoning (recipe on following page)

On the Side

Pita Crisps with Moroccan Seasoning

½	cup (125 mL) butter, at room temperature
2	teaspoons (10 mL) Moroccan rub seasoning (see tip)
9	(about 7-inch/18 cm) pita breads
	Coarse sea salt

In small bowl, mix butter and Moroccan rub seasoning until well blended.

Half pita breads by inserting tip of scissors into edge of each pita; cut along edge to separate into 2 rounds. Spread smooth side of each pita round with scant ½ tablespoon (7 mL) seasoned butter. Cut each round into 8 wedges. Place buttered-side up on ungreased rimmed baking sheet.

Bake at 375 F (190 C) for 6 to 8 minutes or until golden and crisp. Sprinkle with salt to taste. Transfer pita crisps to rack and let cool. *(Make ahead: Place crisps in airtight container and store for up to 5 days at room temperature or freeze for up to 2 weeks.)*

Tips

• *We used a Moroccan rub called NOMU. This rub is a blend of seasonings containing cumin, sugar, coriander, salt, black pepper, parsley, chili, cinnamon, turmeric, ginger, nutmeg, cloves, cardamom, coriander leaves and orange oil.*

• *These versatile pita crisps can be sprinkled with just about any seasoning blend that you like. Experiment and introduce your palate to exotic and international flavourings by using different spice blends and rubs like Egyptian dukka, smoky peri-peri or za'atar.*

Makes 72 crisps. PER CRISP: 35 cal, 1 g pro, 2 g fat, 5 g carb.

Red Onion Focaccia (Bread Machine)

Dough

1	cup (250 mL) water, at room temperature
¼	cup (50 mL) extra-virgin olive oil
1½	teaspoons (7 mL) salt
2¼	cups (550 mL) all-purpose flour
⅓	cup (75 mL) yellow cornmeal
2	teaspoons (10 mL) granulated sugar
2	teaspoons (10 mL) bread machine yeast
2	teaspoons (10 mL) chopped fresh oregano
1	teaspoon (5 mL) chopped fresh rosemary

Topping

3	tablespoons (45 mL) extra-virgin olive oil, divided
1¼	cups (300 mL) thinly sliced red onion
2	tablespoons (30 mL) fresh whole rosemary leaves
	Salt and pepper

Dough: Add dough ingredients to bread machine pan in order recommended by machine's manufacturer. Select dough/manual cycle.

Meanwhile prepare topping: In small heavy frypan, heat 2 tablespoons (30 mL) oil over medium heat. Add onion; saute for 3 minutes. Add whole rosemary leaves; saute for 1 minute. Set aside.

When dough/manual cycle is complete, transfer dough to lightly floured surface. If necessary, knead in enough flour to make dough easy to handle; cover and let rest for 10 minutes.

Roll dough out into 12-inch (30 cm) circle; place in greased 12-inch (30 cm) pizza pan. Cover and let rise in warm, draft-free place for 15 minutes or until almost doubled in size. With fingertips, press slight indentations into dough. Sprinkle onion mixture evenly over top of dough. Sprinkle with salt and pepper to taste. Drizzle with remaining 1 tablespoon (15 mL) oil. Bake at 400 F (200 C) for 25 to 30 minutes or until baked. Transfer focaccia to rack; let cool slightly. Serve warm.

Makes 8 wedges. PER WEDGE: 262 cal, 5 g pro, 11 g fat, 35 g carb.

Simple-To-Make Puff Pastry Twists

½   cup (125 mL) plus 2 tablespoons (30 mL) finely grated old white cheddar cheese

½   cup (125 mL) plus 2 tablespoons (30 mL) finely grated parmesan cheese

¼   teaspoon (1 mL) Spanish smoked hot paprika or chipotle chili pepper

¼   teaspoon (1 mL) coarse sea salt

1   (397 g) package frozen puff pastry, thawed

     Egg wash (1 egg beaten with 1 teaspoon/5 mL water)

Put cheddar and parmesan cheeses into small bowl. Sprinkle paprika and salt on top; using fork, toss to mix well.

On lightly floured surface, roll half the pastry into 14x6-inch (36x15 cm) rectangle. With short side of pastry closest to you, brush pastry with some of the egg wash to within ¼ inch (5 mm) of edge. Sprinkle pastry evenly with ¼ cup (50 mL) cheese mixture. Gently press cheese mixture into pastry. Fold pastry in half by folding short side of pastry (side closest to you) up to meet other short end of pastry, making a 7x6-inch (18x15 cm) rectangle. Gently press top of pastry. Pinch edges to seal. With sharp knife, trim edges to make an even edge. Lightly brush top with some of the egg wash. Sprinkle evenly with 2 tablespoons (30 mL) cheese mixture, pressing it lightly into pastry.

Cut filled pastry lengthwise into ½-inch (1 cm) wide strips. Holding the end of each strip with fingertips, twist the strip in opposite directions 4 or 5 times, then transfer to ungreased rimmed baking sheet, leaving 1½ inches (4 cm) between strips. To keep strips twisted, press each end down firmly onto baking sheet. Place in refrigerator for 30 minutes.

Bake at 400 F (200 C) for 12 to 15 minutes or until light golden. Let twists cool on baking sheet for 2 minutes; transfer to rack and let cool. Repeat with remaining pastry, cheese mixture and egg wash. *(Make ahead: Place twists in airtight container and freeze for up to 2 weeks.)*

Makes 24 twists. PER TWIST: 94 cal, 3 g pro, 6 g fat, 7 g carb.

Cracked Pepper Bread

2½   cups (625 mL) all-purpose flour
1   cup (250 mL) whole-wheat flour
½   cup (125 mL) quick-cooking oats (not instant)
2   tablespoons (30 mL) packed brown sugar
2   teaspoons (10 mL) baking powder
1   teaspoon (5 mL) baking soda
1   teaspoon (5 mL) salt
½   teaspoon (2 mL) cracked black pepper
2   teaspoons (10 mL) chopped fresh rosemary
1½   cups (375 mL) buttermilk
1   large egg
3   tablespoons (45 mL) vegetable oil
    Egg wash (1 egg beaten with 1 teaspoon/5 mL water)
1   tablespoon (15 mL) quick-cooking oats (not instant)

In large bowl, whisk together all-purpose and whole-wheat flours,
½ cup (125 mL) oats, sugar, baking powder, soda, salt, pepper and
rosemary. In another bowl, whisk together buttermilk, egg and oil.

Make a well in centre of flour mixture. Pour in buttermilk mixture and
quickly stir just until dry ingredients are moistened (do not overmix).
Using hands, bring dough together to form a loose ball. Turn dough out
onto lightly floured surface and knead gently 10 times or until smooth.

Pat dough into 7-inch (18 cm) circle; place on lightly greased, rimless
baking sheet. Using sharp knife, slash top with an X about ½-inch
(1 cm) deep. Lightly brush top of dough with some of the egg wash and
sprinkle with 1 tablespoon (15 mL) oats. Bake at 375 F (190 C) for 35
minutes or until bread sounds hollow when tapped on bottom. Transfer
bread to rack; let cool slightly. Cut bread in half crosswise; place each
half cut side down and cut crosswise into 1-inch (2.5 cm) thick slices.
Serve warm.

Tip: *Omit pepper and rosemary and add ½ cup (125 mL) currants.*

Makes 16 slices. PER SLICE: 149 cal, 5 g pro, 4 g fat, 24 g carb.

Flax Seed Bread (Bread Machine)

1	cup (250 mL) buttermilk
⅔	cup (150 mL) water, at room temperature
2	tablespoons (30 mL) vegetable oil
1	teaspoon (5 mL) salt
3	tablespoons (45 mL) liquid honey
2	cups (500 mL) all-purpose flour
1	cup (250 mL) whole-wheat flour
½	teaspoon (2 mL) baking soda
½	cup (125 mL) ground flax seeds
½	cup (125 mL) oat bran
⅓	cup (75 mL) natural wheat bran
2	tablespoons (30 mL) whole flax seeds
1½	teaspoons (7 mL) bread machine yeast
	Egg wash (1 egg beaten with 1 teaspoon/5 mL water)

Add all ingredients except egg wash to bread machine pan in order recommended by machine's manufacturer. Select dough/manual cycle. When cycle is complete, transfer dough to lightly floured surface. If necessary, knead in enough all-purpose flour to make dough easy to handle; cover and let rest for 15 minutes.

Punch dough down. On lightly floured surface, shape dough into 7-inch (18 cm) round. Place on lightly greased, rimless baking sheet and lightly press top of dough to flatten slightly. Cover and let rise in warm, draft-free place for 30 minutes or until doubled in size.

Using sharp knife, slash top of dough 3 times. Lightly brush top with some of the egg wash. Bake at 375 F (190 C) for 30 minutes or until bread sounds hollow when tapped on bottom. Transfer bread to rack; let cool.

Tip: *To obtain ½ cup (125 mL) ground flax seeds, put 6 tablespoons (90 mL) whole flax seeds in coffee or spice grinder and grind.*

Makes 16 slices. PER SLICE: 142 cal, 5 g pro, 3 g fat, 26 g carb.

Cheddar and Chive Mini Cornmeal Muffins

½	cup (125 mL) yellow cornmeal
½	cup (125 mL) all-purpose flour
1	tablespoon (15 mL) granulated sugar
¼	teaspoon (1 mL) baking powder
⅛	teaspoon (0.5 mL) baking soda
¼	teaspoon (1 mL) salt
¼	cup (50 mL) buttermilk
2	tablespoons (30 mL) extra-virgin olive oil
1	large egg
¾	cup (175 mL) canned cream-style corn
2	tablespoons (30 mL) chopped fresh chives
1	tablespoon (15 mL) chopped, drained sun-dried tomatoes (oil-packed)
¼	cup (50 mL) finely chopped red onion
¼	cup (50 mL) grated old white cheddar cheese

In large bowl, whisk together cornmeal, flour, sugar, baking powder, soda and salt.

In medium bowl, whisk together buttermilk, oil and egg. Whisk in corn until well blended. Whisk in chives and sun-dried tomatoes.

Make a well in centre of cornmeal mixture. Pour in buttermilk mixture and quickly stir just until dry ingredients are moistened (do not overmix).

Spoon batter into 24 greased (1¾-inch/4 cm) mini muffin cups. Sprinkle each muffin with a level ½ teaspoon (2 mL) each of onion and cheese.

Bake at 400 F (200 C) for 15 to 18 minutes or until top springs back when lightly pressed in centre and edges are golden. Remove muffins from pan and let cool slightly on rack. Serve warm.

Tips

• *Half a (398 mL) can cream-style corn yields ¾ cup (175 mL).*

• *The secret to making tender muffins and other quick breads is to quickly mix the wet and dry ingredients until just moistened (the batter should look lumpy). Overmixing will result in a tough texture.*

• *Cast-Iron Frypan variation: Lightly brush 10-inch (25 cm) cast-iron frypan (diameter of the bottom of frypan is about 8½-inches/22 cm) with olive oil. Preheat frypan in 400 F (200 C) oven for 10 minutes. Double the mini muffin recipe ingredients. Slice the onion instead of finely chopping it.*

Pour batter into preheated cast-iron frypan. Sprinkle evenly with onion and cheese. Bake for 30 to 35 minutes. Let cornbread stand in frypan on rack for 10 minutes; using a non-scratch utensil, cut into wedges.

• *Baking Pan variation: Double the mini muffin recipe ingredients. Slice the onion instead of finely chopping it. Pour batter into greased 9-inch (23 cm) square baking pan. Sprinkle evenly with onion and cheese. Bake for 35 to 40 minutes. Let cornbread stand in pan on rack for 10 minutes, then cut into 12 squares.*

• *Standard-Size Muffin Cup variation: Double the mini muffin recipe ingredients. Chop red onion but not as finely as for the mini-muffins. Spoon batter into 12 greased standard-size muffin cups. Sprinkle each with an equal portion of the onion and cheese. Bake for 25 minutes.*

Makes 24 mini muffins. PER MUFFIN: 49 cal, 1 g pro, 2 g fat, 7 g carb.

Beaufort Cheese Scones

2	cups (500 mL) all-purpose flour
2	teaspoons (10 mL) baking powder
¼	teaspoon (1 mL) baking soda
½	teaspoon (2 mL) salt
¼	teaspoon (1 mL) dry mustard
¼	teaspoon (1 mL) Spanish smoked hot paprika
½	cup (125 mL) cold butter, cut into small pieces
1½	cups (375 mL) grated Beaufort or old white cheddar cheese, divided
¼	cup (50 mL) finely chopped fresh chives
1	large egg
½	cup (125 mL) plus 2 tablespoons (30 mL) buttermilk

In large bowl, whisk together flour, baking powder, soda, salt, mustard and paprika. Using pastry blender, cut in butter until mixture resembles coarse crumbs. Stir in 1 cup (250 mL) cheese and chives.

In small bowl, whisk egg: whisk in buttermilk until well blended. Add buttermilk mixture, all at once, to flour mixture and stir with a fork, adding a little additional buttermilk, if necessary, to form a soft dough. Using hands, bring dough together in bowl.

Turn dough out onto lightly floured surface and gently knead 10 times or until it forms a cohesive mass. Pat dough into 7½-inch (19 cm) circle, about ¾-inch (2 cm) thick; cut into 8 wedges. Place scones on parchment-paper-lined or ungreased rimless baking sheet; sprinkle each scone with an equal portion of the remaining ½ cup (125 mL) cheese. Bake at 400 F (200 C) for 15 to 17 minutes or until golden. Transfer scones to rack and let cool slightly. Serve warm.

Tip: *Beaufort cheese is a hard, cow's-milk cheese with a fruity aroma and nutty sharp flavour. If your specialty cheese shop doesn't carry it, substitute a premium-quality, old white cheddar.*

Makes 8 scones. PER SCONE: 336 cal, 11 g pro, 21 g fat, 27 g carb.

Garlic Croutes

16   (½-inch/1 cm thick) baguette slices
2   garlic cloves
2   tablespoons (30 mL) extra-virgin olive oil

Place baguette slices on ungreased rimmed baking sheet. Broil both sides of the bread for 1 to 2 minutes or until golden. Rub 1 side of each baguette slice with garlic clove, then brush lightly with some of the oil.

Makes 16 croutes. PER 2 CROUTES: 59 cal, 1 g pro, 2 g fat, 8 g carb.

Rosemary Croutons

2   tablespoons (30 mL) extra-virgin olive oil
1   teaspoon (5 mL) chopped fresh rosemary
4   cups (1 L) cubed (¾-inch/2 cm) day-old sourdough bread

In large bowl, whisk together oil and rosemary. Add bread cubes; toss. Place, in single layer, on ungreased rimmed baking sheet. Bake at 375 F (190 C) for 10 to 15 minutes or until golden and crisp, stirring twice. Let croutons cool on sheet on rack. *(Make ahead: Put croutons in airtight container and store at room temperature for up to 3 days.)*

Per ¼-cup (50 mL) serving: 46 cal, 1 g pro, 2 g fat, 6 g carb.

Index

About The Nutritional Analysis

- The approximate nutritional analysis for each recipe does not include variations or optional ingredients. Figures are rounded off.
- Abbreviations: cal = calories, pro = protein, carb = carbohydrate
- The analysis is based on the first ingredient listed where there is a choice.

SOCCER STAR!

SOCCER STAR!

Jacqueline Guest

James Lorimer & Company Ltd., Publishers
Toronto

James Lorimer & Company Ltd. acknowledges the support of the Ontario Arts Council. We acknowledge the support of the Government of Canada through the Book Publishing Industry Development Program (BPIDP) for our publishing activities. We acknowledge the support of the Canada Council for the Arts for our publishing program. We acknowledge the support of the Government of Ontario through the Ontario Media Development Corporation's Ontario Book Initiative.

Library and Archives Canada Cataloguing in Publication
Guest, Jacqueline
Soccer Star! / Jacqueline Guest.

(Sports stories)
ISBN 978-1-55277-510-3

I. Title. II. Series: Sports stories (Toronto, Ont.)

PS8563.U365S62 2010   jC813'.54   C2010-900289-X

James Lorimer & Company Ltd.,
Publishers
317 Adelaide St. West
Suite 1002
Toronto, Ontario
M5V 1P9
www.lorimer.ca

Distributed in the United States by:
Orca Book Publishers
P.O. Box 468
Custer, WA USA
98240-0468

Printed and bound in Canada.
Manufactured by Friesens Corporation in Altona, Manitoba, Canada in February 2010. Job # 53495

CONTENTS

For Eleanor, with love

Remembering snowy afternoons of baking cookies,
long evenings of secrets shared,
and days made brighter by your smile.

Author's Note

Meet Samantha Aqsarniq Keyes.

Sam's mother is from Nunavut, the newest territory in Canada. Nunavut means "our land" in Inuktitut, the language spoken by those who live in the eastern part of Canada's far north.

Sam's Inuk name, Aqsarniq, was inspired by a legend about the northern lights (also known as "aurora borealis"), the bright dancing colours that fill the northern sky with an eerie glow. The story goes that the strands of light represent the souls of the dead playing a game of celestial soccer. I thought this was the perfect name for a girl who wants to be a soccer star.

I would like to thank Captain Veronica van Diepen, Public Affairs Officer at Canadian Forces Base Edmonton Garrison, and Daniel Burgess of Arviat, Nunavut, for their valuable help in the writing of this book.

— *Jacqueline Guest*
www.jacquelineguest.com

1 WHOLE NEW GAME

It was coming out of the sun straight for her. Samantha squinted, and tried to judge when the soccer ball would be at the exact height she needed. To score, she would have to get it past the two defensive players who were covering her so closely. Positioning her head as her coach instructed, Sam sprang into the air. She felt the power of a solid hit as her forehead connected with the upper half of the ball. Eyes on the goal line, she directed the ball downward.

The keeper never saw it coming. It was a clean win for the Gagetown Beasts. Sam grinned at her teammates and accepted their slaps on the back. She didn't like to be the centre of attention, but after scoring the winning goal it's hard to stay out of the limelight. The fans were still cheering wildly as the team came off the field.

Sam really wanted to win this game; it was her last match in New Brunswick. Tomorrow, she and her family were flying to their new home at Edmonton Garrison in Alberta. Sam's mom was a Warrant Officer in the Lord Strathcona's Horse and commanded a Leopard C2 tank. Quite a mouthful for a thirteen-year-old, but Sam was used to life in the Canadian Armed Forces. Each year brought new places, new people, and new teams. She'd been playing soccer for six years and loved the game no matter where she lived.

Sam spotted her family walking across the penalty area. Her mom waved and smiled warmly. She'd come directly from work and still wore her uniform. Beneath her special black beret, her long dark hair was pulled back in a tidy bun.

"Great job, *Paniq*!" her mom said, using the pet name she'd called Sam since she was a young girl. *Paniq* means *daughter* in Inuktitut. Sam's mom was an Inuk from Arviat, Nunavut, the newest territory in Canada. She'd met Sam's dad when she'd been stationed in Petawawa, Ontario. He was a freelance sports reporter and said he could work anywhere he could plug in his computer. He also coached her big brother, Jordan, at wrestling and would start a club wherever they were stationed.

The family didn't get back up north to visit often, but when they did, it was a celebration. Sam's *ananatsiaq*, which means *grandmother*, was one of the wisest people Sam had ever met. She was full of stories about living out *on the land*, the frozen tundra that went on for thousands of kilometres.

Sam was proud of her Inuit heritage. In fact, the family had decided to incorporate her mom's Inuit family name, *Aqsarniq*, with her dad's, which was why she had such a fancy name, Samantha Aqsarniq Keyes. Her brother, Jordan, had shortened it to *Sam* because he thought it sounded more like a soccer jock.

"I'm glad you caught the game, Mom." Sam wiped the well-earned sweat off her forehead. "Pulling off a hat trick is always neat."

She tilted her head self-consciously. She didn't usually brag about her playing, but three goals deserved a pat on the back. On the field, Sam was filled with girl power and could outplay anyone, but off the field, she turned into another person. Her brother said she wouldn't say "boo" to a mouse if she caught it stealing her cheese.

"Not bad for a girl," Jordan said, punching her on the shoulder. "Now if only you weren't so ugly."

Sam looked down at her worn cleats, trying to ignore her brother's teasing. If he stopped bugging her, she'd probably wonder what was wrong with him, but it still hurt.

Her dad ruffled her hair. "You really are a great soccer player, Sam. I'm glad we could squeeze in this last game." He glanced at his watch. "I'm afraid we'll have to get moving if we're going to finish packing."

Sam looked over at her teammates and felt a pang of regret. "Let me get my stuff. The girls gave me a going-away present and I want to say goodbye."

As she headed for the bench, Sam thought of the photo album her teammates had given her. It was filled with pictures of the team doing what they loved most — playing soccer. She was going to miss them. She hated goodbyes, and she'd had a lot of them.

★ ★ ★

Sam tightened her seat belt and waited as the jet landed with a thump. She'd been leafing through a new magazine and had made a mental list of the clothes she'd like to buy, if only she had a million dollars. Also, a new haircut might be fun to try. Her thick, straight black hair was pulled back in a ponytail that didn't suit her round face. She'd never really cared before, but ever since she turned thirteen, Sam felt it was time for a change.

She went back to the magazine. She'd been avidly following the lives of several young actresses whose stories she found fascinating. For months Sam had been dreaming about what it would be like to star in a movie. One day, maybe, she'd find out.

"Come on, Sam, get your head out of the clouds." Her dad was gathering their carry-on luggage. "A new adventure is waiting right outside that door." He nodded to the exit and winked at her. "Not to mention a new soccer team."

Sam took a last glimpse at her magazine, then tucked it reluctantly into her backpack and followed him off the plane.

★ ★ ★

They were moving to a part of the Edmonton Garrison called Lancaster Park. Sam had expected their house at the PMQs, or Permanent Married Quarters, to be the same as on every other base: drab green, square, and two stories, with one sickly tree in the front yard and a bunch of kids racing around. She was surprised to see tree-lined streets and well-tended gardens instead.

Sam smiled when she saw that they lived on Flanders Avenue. Every base had a Flanders Avenue or an Ortona Road, and lots of other street names that commemorated the Canadian battles of the Second World War.

"I've got one stop to make before we get to our new house," Sam's dad said. "But you kids need to know where this particular building is anyway." He turned into the parking lot of a sleek new complex.

"Lancaster Park School." Sam read the sign on the building. "Wow! This place is huge."

"You'll start here on Monday," he went on. "Right now, I want to check on the arrangements for the wrestling group I'm going to teach here after school." He parked the car and hurried into the building while the rest of the family waited outside.

"Why don't we have a look around," Sam's mom suggested, as she climbed out of the car.

"Not me, I'm going to snooze," Jordan said. He hunkered down in his seat, and pulled his ball cap over his eyes.

Sam followed her mother, thinking she may as well get the lay of the land. She wandered toward a notice board near the school entrance. As she scanned the announcements, a bright pink sheet caught her eye.

It was a review of the Lancaster Drama Club's last play, which had apparently been a hit. There were pictures of actors in wonderful costumes, and the sets looked fantastic. At the bottom of the poster a notice read: "*Watch for our next extravaganza at a theatre near you.*" Sam felt a shiver of excitement. Maybe she could be a part of that new extravaganza?

Then she frowned. Her parents had a rule that she could join only one extracurricular activity. This came about after Sam had made some poor time-management choices. Her grades had taken a nosedive and she'd needed extra tutoring in math to get back up to speed. The good news was that, because of the tutoring, Sam was now a math whiz. For the past few years, she'd always chosen soccer as her activity.

But what if Lancaster Park didn't have a soccer team? What if she joined the Drama Club instead? Her parents' rule didn't say her one activity had to be sports. Would she have the courage to do drama? The thought of getting up in front of a crowd to perform was both thrilling and terrifying. When Sam was on a soccer field she never worried about the crowds, she was too focused. Maybe it would be the same with acting; maybe she could have this dream. The possibility made her stomach flip-flop.

"Paniq, come over here," her mom called excitedly. "Look at this!"

As Sam walked toward her mother, her eyes were drawn to the open grass field. Silhouetted against the early evening sky was a blonde girl about Sam's age kicking a soccer ball.

2 NEW SCHOOL BLUES

Sam wondered how, after all the schools she had attended, she could still be nervous on her first day. She hated the knot she felt in her stomach when she met new people. She'd promised herself this time that she was going to be a new Sam, brave and fearless.

She stood in front of her closet trying to decide what to wear. It had to be something cool to reflect her new attitude. Unfortunately her clothes, mostly jeans and T-shirts, all looked like last year's models. It would have been nice to have something new, blue and perhaps miniskirtish for her first day. She picked out a pair of jeans and a baggy orange hoodie with a reflective number eighteen on the front.

One recent improvement was that Sam's parents had finally let her get contact lenses to replace her clunky glasses. She had chosen a shade of green that she thought made her look mysterious and exotic. She'd also stopped at the Canex, which was the military version of a department store, and bought some green eyeshadow and pink lipstick to go with her new look.

"Ow!" Sam gritted her teeth. She was still having trouble putting the filmy lenses into her eyes. "Now to top off the new look," she said to her reflection in the mirror, "a dab of this and a dash of that." She was putting the finishing touches on her makeup when Jordan walked by her room.

"Hey, I didn't think Halloween was until October! You should take off that mask before you freak someone out!" He belched loudly, howled with laughter, and continued down the hall.

Sam's confidence in her new look evaporated. "As if!" she squeaked, but her brother was already out of earshot.

Sam wasn't experienced with makeup yet and had been using a picture out of her magazine as a model. When she studied her face in the mirror, her heart sank. The heavy mascara looked like a couple of tarantulas hanging off her eyelids, and the eyeshadow made her appear as though she'd been on the losing end of a fight. How did her lipstick end up so bright? And now the pink goop was smeared across her front teeth.

This definitely wasn't the look she was going for. Sam sighed, headed for the bathroom, grabbed a washcloth and scrubbed her face. So much for Sam, Exotic Woman of Mystery.

Still, she couldn't go to school on her first day looking ordinary. These kids were going to meet a new Sam, and she wanted to look the part. She glanced around her room for some way to spruce up her look. A pretty pink barrette sat next to a pile of books on her dresser. Sam grabbed it and pinned back her hair. As she did, she caught sight of her *inuksuk* on the windowsill. It had been a gift from her mom and was one of Sam's favourite things.

The sun shining on the small sculpture made her feel at home in her new room. Sam's mom said the word *inuksuk* means "something that can act in the place of a human being." The stone markers were signposts for the Inuit people, who traditionally spent their lives travelling great distances. Sam's *inuksuk* was an *Inunnguaq*, which meant *like a person* because of its shape. *Inunnguaq* were made of flat pieces of rock stacked like books and looked like men with heads, bodies, legs and arms that stood straight out from their sides.

The statue made Sam feel brave again. She smiled at her *inuksuk*, then took one last look at herself in the mirror. "Ready or not, Lancaster Park," she whispered. "Here I come!"

★ ★ ★

Sam scanned her new classroom for a place to sit. This late in the year, the only empty desks would be among the geeks. She sighed and headed toward the back. As she passed a group of girls chatting and giggling, she recognized one of them as the blonde girl she saw on the soccer field yesterday.

"*Settle!*" commanded a voice like a drill sergeant's.

Sam turned her attention toward the jumbo-sized figure filling the doorway. Mrs. Steele, her new math teacher, was built like a tank, with iron-grey hair and thick black eyebrows that looked like they'd been drawn on with a magic marker.

Sam slipped into a desk next to a nerd who wore a short-sleeved white shirt buttoned right up to the collar. He sat at full attention. Class began.

"Today we have a new student joining us. Ms. Samantha Aqsarniq Keyes, please stand up," boomed Mrs. Steele.

Sam felt like a contestant in a game show as she slowly got to her feet. She could feel every eye on her, and her face burned with embarrassment. Off to one side, she saw the blonde turn and whisper to a redhead sitting beside her. From the confident way she tossed her long, stylish hair and how everyone had said "hi" to her when they came in, she was obviously the most popular girl here.

The blonde was wearing a navy top with a French designer's name across the front and matching mini-skirt. Sam's spirits slumped. Her brother had been right about the Halloween look — compared to this girl, she felt like a huge pumpkin in her orange hoodie.

Math class went downhill from there. They were

working on some tricky algebra problems when Mrs. Steele came and stood behind Sam's desk, surveying her notebook. The hairs on the back of Sam's neck stood at attention. She glanced over at the blonde, who was again whispering with a friend.

"*Ms. Carly Gibson!*"

Sam jumped, breaking her pencil point.

The blonde froze. "Since you're talking," said Mrs. Steele, "I assume you're finished the problems. Do Question Three on the board."

Sam knew how this Carly girl must have felt at that moment. Nothing was worse than getting up in front of your classmates to do a math problem. Before her tutoring, she couldn't do math to save her life. Even now, she hated being singled out in front of the class. It was like facing a firing squad. Sam wondered if Carly Gibson wanted a blindfold.

"Actually, Mrs. Steele, I didn't get that one," Carly said.

"Well, in that case, why don't you show us all where you're having your *difficulties.*" The math teacher sucked air between her teeth like a dragon inhaling.

Carly walked to the board and picked up a piece of chalk. Slowly, she began the steps toward solving the problem. Unfortunately, after the first two, she made a mistake. Sam groaned inwardly. The girl was doomed.

After watching Carly battle with the problem for another five minutes, the dragon became irritated. Sam saw Carly's face redden as she struggled.

"*Samantha Aqsarniq Keyes!*" Again, Sam jumped. "Please assist Ms. Gibson with her *difficulties.*"

Sam hesitated. Showing up the most popular girl in class was no way to make friends, but she had no choice. The dragon had seen the completed problem in Sam's workbook.

As Sam made her way to the board, she undid her pink barrette so that her hair hung around her face. She didn't want to look at anyone and she sure didn't want anyone looking at her. She erased most of what Carly had struggled with, causing the class to erupt into giggles, then quickly solved the problem and retreated to her seat.

"Commendable, Ms. Aqsarniq Keyes," Mrs. Steele said, sealing Sam's position with the geeks. Sam kept her eyes on her workbook. She could feel Carly glaring at her.

No one spoke to Sam at the end of the class. Carly and her fans looked over at her, then broke out in snickers. Sam headed for the hallway, wishing she were invisible.

To her surprise, when Sam arrived at her locker, Carly and three of her friends were waiting. A cute guy also stood with them.

Sam was confused. Was she forgiven for the math fiasco? Was this guy some kind of peace offering? Her spirits rose for an instant, then she realized they weren't there to welcome her at all. Carly's locker was next to Sam's.

Sam remembered her promise to be brave. Despite this morning's *difficulties*, maybe it wasn't too late to make some new friends. She put on her best smile and walked up to the group.

"Hi! I'm Sam," she said brightly.

The group stopped talking and turned to her. "We know," Carly said. The four girls chimed in singsong unison, "*Ms. Samantha Aqsarniq Keyes.*"

"Right," Sam said, pulling on her locker door. It was jammed shut, and she felt her face getting warm. "That's me." She finally managed to free the door and began stuffing her books into the locker.

"Hi Samantha Aqsarniq Keyes. I'm Josh Carter. Welcome to the jungle."

Josh Carter had the most amazing smile she'd ever seen. What a *hottie!* A moment passed before she realized she was staring. Pulling herself together, she noticed a sheaf of papers under Josh's arm. One word caught her eye: "Auditions."

"You're with the Lancaster Drama Club?" she spluttered. It sounded more like an accusation than a question.

"Oh, yeah!" Josh said in a voice rich as melted chocolate. "Best school drama club in all of Edmonton, maybe Alberta!"

Sam felt her legs go wobbly. "I'm really interested

in acting, but I've never had the chance to try it." She knew she sounded star-struck, but she didn't want to let the subject drop.

"Then this is your lucky day." Josh handed her one of the posters. It read:

AUDITIONS
The Lancaster Drama Club announces auditions for
"Romeo Dude and Julie Baby,"
stolen from Bill Shakespeare
Monday, 4:00 p.m., in the Auditorium
No experience necessary

Sam looked up into Josh's smiling face and couldn't help smiling back.

"I'd better get to my next class. Nice to meet you, Samantha Aqsarniq Keyes." Josh turned to the other girls, who were now all staring. "See you tomorrow, Carly."

Carly flashed him a brilliant smile, then teased, "It will be the high point of my day, Josh."

Sam tried to recover some part of her missing brain. She felt like she'd been on the world's fastest roller-coaster ride. Slowly, Sam turned back to her locker and tried to refocus.

"… And remember, in soccer the goalie is the only player who can ever handle the ball. It's hands off for everyone else," she heard Carly say.

"Unless it's a free kick on goal from ten yards away and you're in the wall defending," Sam said without thinking, as she slammed her locker door shut. "Then you can use your hands to protect your chest, or if you're a guy, other sensitive areas."

Silence.

Carly whirled around and glared at her. "I'm talking about regular play. Of course it's okay if you're in a wall and deflecting a ball kicked right at your boobs!"

"Sorry," Sam said. "It's just that, well, you said 'ever' and technically it is legal to touch the ball in a wall formation if you're protecting yourself …"

Carly's eyes narrowed. "Oh, I forgot. You're Ms. Samantha Aqsarniq Keyes, resident math star and now soccer star, too."

Her voice had a dangerous-sounding edge to it. Sam decided to steer the conversation back to friendlier ground. "I saw you practicing on the field yesterday. Great dribbling."

Carly tossed her hair over her shoulder, still angry.

"She's practically captain of the Lancaster Lions," the red-headed girl piped up. "It's the best soccer team in the league."

"I play too." Sam tried to sound confident. "I was thinking about joining the team."

Carly scoffed. "For your information, the season has already started and it's too late to join any team. Go find something else to be a star at." And with that, Carly grabbed her backpack and flounced down the hallway. The other girls immediately followed their leader, leaving Sam standing alone.

Sam was stung by Carly's nastiness, but it was true. The season was well under way. She already had tonnes of practices and had played two games back in Gagetown before her family moved. It was an unexpected problem because her family had never been transferred this close to the end of the school year before. This could be her first year in many without soccer. She couldn't imagine it.

Sam looked down at the paper clenched in her hand. "No experience necessary," it said. No soccer meant she still had an opening for *one extracurricular activity*. She folded the audition poster and tucked it into her back pocket as she headed for class.

3 NEW GAME

There was a sign posted on the auditorium door: "Auditions today. Go to backstage area." Sam took a deep breath — this was the first step in her career as an actor. When it came to marching onto a soccer field, Sam had no fear; stepping into the cavernous theatre was something else. She was so nervous she thought she might faint.

It took her eyes a moment to adjust to the dim light. She noticed several people sitting in the audience, watching a girl about Sam's age reading a scene on the stage.

Quietly, Sam made her way to the stairs leading backstage. Fumbling in the darkness, she missed the first step. Her feet flew out from under her as she crashed noisily down the stairs.

"Hold it, everyone!" A teacher's voice called from the audience. "Will someone please assist the acrobat at the front!"

Sam groaned. This wasn't how her acting career

was supposed to begin. Hands reached out to her, helping her up the stairs and through the door. She was plunked unceremoniously into an old wooden chair against the wall.

"Hello again." Sam looked up to see Josh Carter standing over her. "Glad you could 'drop in.'"

Sam wished the floor would open up and swallow her. "I … I came to audition," she said.

"Just in time. You'll be the last person to read." He handed her a script. "We're doing an updated version of Romeo and Juliet called *Romeo Dude and Julie Baby.* It's a spoof that our drama club worked on over the winter."

Sam looked at the lines, unsure of what it all meant.

"Your part is highlighted and I'll read the rest. I'll give you a couple of minutes to go over the lines, then you're on." He pointed to an area behind the curtains. "You can wait back there."

Feeling overwhelmed, Sam walked obediently to where Josh pointed. She looked down at the script. It was the balcony scene where Romeo eavesdrops on Juliet, except this version was a lot different from the original.

The girl who'd been auditioning earlier walked past and picked up her belongings. "I don't think I made the cut," she said, shrugging her shoulders. "I hope you have better luck."

Sam watched her leave and felt so nervous she

thought she might be sick. She began to sweat. As she fanned herself with the script, she noticed someone standing next to her. It was the nerd with the buttoned-up shirt from math class. Something didn't sound right about the words he was mumbling to himself, and then Sam realized what it was. He was reading Juliet's part, or in this version, Julie Baby's. She was going to suggest that perhaps he had the wrong script, when he turned and headed onto the stage.

Sam listened, amazed at how well the guy did. Instead of being flustered by the girl's part, the nerd, whose name turned out to be Sheldon Holmes, did a great job. He clowned around and improvised, and by the time he'd finished everyone in the audience was howling with laughter. Sheldon bowed with a flourish before bounding off the stage. Sam was impressed.

"Samantha Aqsarniq Keyes, you're up!" Josh called.

A tidal wave of stage fright washed over Sam. Her feet were glued to the floor. Why had she ever thought she could do this?

The last time she had been this frightened was when she was a kid, visiting her *ananatsiaq*. Her grandmother wanted her to go out onto the tundra and gather a bouquet of purple saxifrage, the beautiful official wild-flower of Nunavut. The tundra was vast and desolate, and Sam had been terrified of getting lost. Her grandmother suggested she pretend to be a mighty hunter, a *maqaiti*, afraid of nothing. Sam reluctantly did as she was told, and a strange thing happened. She was concentrating so hard on hunting the caribou, which was actually the purple saxifrage, that she forgot her fear and began to see how beautiful the tundra was. After that day, Sam had never been afraid to go out on the land again.

She took a deep breath, and decided to pretend the stage was just another tundra. She was a mighty hunter, right? Sam stepped into the dazzling light. Feeling faint, she squinted into the darkness, and tried to see the figures in the audience.

"Hey, what's that crazy light I see in the window? Could it be Julie Baby, the hottest babe in the kingdom?" Josh read the lines and waited.

Sam froze. The highlighted lines of her script now resembled a handful of squirming glow worms. She fought a strong urge to drop the pages and run away. Josh nodded encouragingly, seeming to understand her confusion.

"Could it be *Samantha* Baby, the hottest babe in the kingdom?" Josh repeated with a grin.

His use of her name turned a switch on in her brain. Sam looked down at the script again. The worms were gone and in their place were nice, easy-to-read words. She felt like a hunter, not a mighty one, but a hunter! "Romeo Dude, hey Romeo Dude, where are you hanging these days, you fine lookin' thing?"

Slowly, Sam relaxed. Josh kept encouraging her, and by the time the reading ended she was getting into the part, using body gestures and facial expressions to add flare. It was fun pretending to be someone completely different, someone other than Samantha Aqsarniq Keyes.

When she finished, she turned to face the darkness. There was dead silence. "Was that ... okay?" she asked. No one said anything. Her spirits sank. Sam rolled up her script and headed off the stage.

"Thank you — Samantha, is it?" a voice from the darkness asked. Sam turned and nodded. "Please wait backstage with the rest of the cast. Josh, could you come here?"

Sam did as she was told. After an eternity, Josh rejoined her.

"All the actors will be officially notified of their parts later, but right now, take a bow, Samantha. We've found our 'Julie Baby.'" He gave her a hug that left Sam's knees weak. "That person who told you to wait was Mr. Bidwell, the director," he explained. "Man, you really blew him away." Josh handed her a copy of the complete script. "He wants to get started this week. See you on Saturday, Samantha."

Sam floated all the way home. She had done it. She'd auditioned for her first part and the director had loved her. She was going to be an actor!

★ ★ ★

That night at supper, Sam waited for the perfect moment to break the bad news about soccer and the amazing news about the play. She was still tingling with the excitement of the audition.

"How did everyone's first day go?" her mom asked. She knew how tough it was to change schools. You spent the first couple of weeks catching up on what you hadn't learned in your old school, while trying to fit in with kids who didn't want a stranger butting into their group.

"My classes are way tough," Jordan began, and Sam knew he was setting up his excuse for the slumping grades he anticipated. He was always popular wherever they moved. Until this year, he'd been able to keep his marks up while participating in lots of outside activities. Before they left New Brunswick, though, Sam noticed he was getting a lot of calls from girls who wanted him to join this club or go to that dance.

"I've got a math teacher who's an ex-drill sergeant," Sam said. "She gives teachers a bad name."

She was dying to tell everyone about the play, but timing was everything. She wanted all the usual dinner conversation to be over before her big announcement. In the meantime she spooned mashed potatoes onto her plate, making sure there was no room left for any of the loathsome Brussels sprouts that were heaped in a nearby bowl.

Sam thought about the special "Country Food,"

or food from the land, they ate when they visited her grandmother. They had dishes like *Maktaaq*, Beluga whale blubber, and even Head and Hoof Soup, which was made from caribou and often still had some fur on it. Her grandmother loved the eyeballs, which were considered a delicacy, while Sam ate the spongy tongue. She remembered her *ananatsiaq's* wrinkled old face grinning at her as she offered Sam *quak*, frozen raw caribou meat. Sam looked at the slimy Brussels sprouts again and wrinkled her nose. She'd gladly trade them in for a bowl of Head and Hoof soup.

"Did you find out about the soccer team?" her mom asked, ignoring the carefully contoured expanse of potatoes on Sam's plate as she made room for a spoonful of the dreaded vegetables.

"Actually," Sam began, "the season's too far along and I won't be able to join the team." She took a deep breath and sighed disappointedly. She actually was. Not playing soccer was going to be strange. "I guess I'll have to find something else to do."

Her family looked shocked.

"No soccer, that bites!" Jordan exclaimed.

"That's terrible news," her mom said. "I'm sorry to hear that, Paniq."

Sam's dad didn't say anything.

"Whatever happens, remember, when you're signing up for extracurricular activities, pick *one*." Her mom gave her a meaningful look.

Sam felt her brows draw together. "I *know*, Mom."

"Hey, speaking of your old screw-ups, whatever happened to that violin you *had* to have, Sam?" Jordan mumbled, his mouth so full of Brussels sprouts that he looked like his cheeks were packed with marbles. "Man, what a racket you used to make. I was actually glad when you dumped that expensive little experiment." He swallowed noisily.

Sam glared at her brother. He never let her forget how much money it had cost for her to try out her various short-lived interests.

"And I know hockey is big in Edmonton," Jordan continued as though his mouth had no dribble control. "You could try selling all that hockey equipment we've been hauling around. At least when you were going to be an Olympic swimmer, there wasn't much leftover junk."

Sam could feel her face flushing. She couldn't help it if she'd changed her mind. Those things just weren't right for her.

"That's enough Jordan," Sam's mother said firmly. "You've made your point, and I don't expect any problems with your sister and whatever activity she chooses. I hope I can say the same about you and your wrestling." This last comment shut Mr. Big Mouth up. Everyone at the table knew Jordan's marks had started to slip.

Sam decided that now was the perfect time to tell her family about the play. She was about to open her mouth when her dad put down his knife and fork and smiled broadly at Sam.

"Sam will play soccer," he said. "Not only does she love the sport, but she's good at it."

"Thanks Dad, but as I explained, I'm too late."

"I heard the same thing from the gym teacher at school today. Well, your old dad couldn't let his little girl miss playing her favourite game, so I went to the coach, great guy by the name of Dearing, and we had a little chat — one coach to another."

Sam was now on full alert.

"I pulled some strings, told him how good you are and — presto — *you're in!* You start with your new team, the Lancaster Lions, tomorrow. And to celebrate …" He rummaged under the table and brought out a box. "Happy early birthday Sam!" Both parents beamed at her.

Sam took the box and opened it apprehensively. "Wow, new soccer cleats." She tried to sound enthusiastic. They were a very expensive brand. "Thanks Dad and Mom, but you didn't have to do this."

"We talked it over and decided that since you've shown you can stick with something, we would spend the extra money on really good shoes," Sam's mom said. "With your birthday coming up, we thought this was the perfect present."

Her parents were so excited, Sam didn't have the heart to tell them about the drama club. In a perfect world she could do both. She was sure she was old enough to handle two extracurricular activities, and she'd been excited ever since the auditions. But Sam's mom was a stickler for rules and there was no way she'd let Sam do drama now, not after all the trouble they'd gone through to get her on the soccer team.

Forcing a smile, Sam held up her new cleats for everyone to admire.

4 PRACTICE MAKES PERFECT

The next aftearnoon, Sam sat on the grass next to the soccer field beside Lancaster Park School and watched her new teammates as they prepared for practice. She still hadn't figured out how she was going to tell her parents about her acting, especially after their gift.

Sam pulled out her new cleats and admired them. Her old cleats were worn, but she hadn't asked for a new pair because she still felt guilty about all the other things her parents had bought for her. But her parents had faith in her love of soccer. They'd bought the expensive shoes without even a hint from her. Her parents were unbelievably cool. Sam knew what she had to do. She would tell the drama club she couldn't take the part. Maybe next year she would be able to do both soccer *and* drama. Maybe.

Sam got to her feet and headed onto the field just in time to see Carly Gibson kick the ball right through the goalie's legs. Carly's hair was pulled up in a cute ponytail holder with fuzzy feathers that floated when she moved.

Sam took a deep breath and walked up to the bench, where Carly stood taking a drink of water. "Great nutmeg!" she said. It was funny how much easier it was to start a conversation on the soccer field. She wished she could feel this confident all the time.

"What are you doing here? This is a closed practice for Lions players only." Carly took a large gulp of her water, then spit it out onto the ground. The water splatted on the dirt, barely missing Sam's new cleats.

Sam looked down at the mess. This was too much, no drama and now a jerk for a teammate. "That's right and I'm your newest Lion." She took a long pull on her own water bottle and then spit in the direction of Carly's shoes, getting it even closer to the blonde's cleats. Both girls stared at the muddy puddle of water.

"We'll see about *that*!" said Carly, heading over to where Coach Dearing stood writing on his clipboard. After a brief discussion, she stormed back. "The coach says you have 'special circumstances.' Apparently if you know the right people you can break the rules. Let's get something straight. I built this team. Because of me, we're the team everyone wants to beat." Her voice was all business. "What position do you play?"

"Striker." Sam stared defiantly at Carly. She thought the blonde fashion statement looked awfully good for someone who was going to kick a ball around for an hour or two. She was wearing subtle blue eyeshadow, and Sam was sure her lips weren't usually that particular shade of pink.

Carly's eyes narrowed. "Forward, huh? Well, so am I. Highest scorer on our team." And with that, she kicked the ball at Sam, who instantly brought her knee up, pointed her toe and volleyed the ball off her instep and back to Carly. The blonde batted it down with her hand.

"That's because *I* haven't played yet." Sam turned and walked away. Despite her tough talk, she felt sick to her stomach. She hoped she could live up to this boast.

"Ladies," Coach Dearing called. "This is Sam Aqsarniq Keyes, and she'll be joining the Lions as a forward. I'm told by a very good source that she knows her stuff, so it won't take her long to get up to speed." He introduced all the girls, and Sam tried to memorize their names.

"Okay, ladies, let's warm up." Coach Dearing handed out red and blue bibs and divided the team into two squads. Sam got a red one, while Carly had blue. Sam noticed that the girls on the blue squad didn't smile and welcome her like the others.

Sam's eyes fell on the redhead who'd been with Carly at her locker. "Hi. Tara, isn't it?"

Tara nodded, then glanced in Carly's direction. "Don't worry about her. She's kind of stuck up sometimes, but she can really play well. The other girls with her are her 'special friends' and they think anyone who isn't part of their inner circle is a freak." Sam heard the resentment in the girl's voice and figured Tara wasn't part of Carly's inner circle.

The blue squad was laughing and talking as they juggled a ball off their shoes, knees, thighs and foreheads. Sam turned to the red squad. "So how will we warm up?" No one said anything.

Using her instep, Sam flipped a ball up and caught it. When it came to soccer, she wasn't shy at all. "I know a fun dribbling drill called 'Middle Man' we could try." The girls nodded and seemed glad someone was taking over. "Okay, Tara, you're in the middle," Sam glanced over at another of her red teammates, a tall, freckle-faced girl with braids, and smiled.

"S–Stephanie Nimchuk. Steph to my f-f-friends. I'm a m-m-midfielder," the lanky girl stammered.

"Great, Steph. You and I are going to practice passing to Tara. She'll snag the pass and send it back out to each of us, alternating sides." She rolled a second ball back toward her, then picked it up on her laces and flicked it to Steph.

"B–b–both of us at the same time?" Steph asked as she caught the ball.

"I guarantee Tara will be warmed up in no time," Sam laughed. The remaining girls grabbed balls and split into groups. Soon the red squad was practicing passes and taking turns at being in the middle. By the time the coach blew his whistle, all the girls were laughing and well warmed up. Carly's squad gave them cold looks as they took their places for a short scrimmage.

Coach Dearing pointed at Sam and Carly. "Call it,

Carly." Sam watched as the coin spun high in the air, glinting in the afternoon sunshine.

"Heads!" Carly said as the coach caught the coin.

"Heads it is."

Carly and her blue squad moved to the half-line, with Sam and her group facing them. Carly kicked a nice punt. Immediately the other blue forward, a girl with curly brown hair named Tammy Cornell, snagged the ball and began dribbling toward the red goal.

Sam knew right away this was no ordinary scrimmage. Carly and her squad played as though it were the closing minutes of the World Cup. They used one-touch passing, give-and-goes and lots of driven passes that moved the ball downfield fast. They were also great at shielding. Sam seemed to be mostly defending, which was not how she played soccer. She was a striker, a finisher, a goal scorer.

When the whistle blew to end the first half, Sam knew her squad was outgunned. They tried hard, but they weren't at the same level of play that Carly and her friends were. Sam, who always believed in playing the best game that she could, decided to make a few suggestions.

"Hey, I'm new here and I don't want to step on anybody's laces, but I have a few plays I used with my last team that might give us an edge with these blue devils." She nodded toward Carly's squad, which was forming up for the second half of the mini-game.

"We'll never beat Carly and her goons," Tara said, wiping her face with a towel. "Charlotte Dorn is a wicked goalie." She tossed the towel down.

"I noticed their goalie has great hands." Sam frowned. "We need to get the darn ball, then we can play keep-away too. You girls are good at dribbling; you just never get a chance. I've got some moves they might not have seen. What if we try this ..." Sam relayed a couple of strategies she had picked up from the Gagetown Beasts. "And in case we get blitzed again, let's try tighter funnelling when we move back to defend our goal. If they can't get past us, they can't score."

They formed back up opposite Carly's blue squad at the half-line. Sam kicked off and passed to Tara, who headed for the goal, but was soon poke-tackled and lost possession. It was a long, painful time before the red team regained the ball — the moment Sam had been waiting for.

"Let's do it!" she called, as Tara dribbled the ball past a couple of blue midfielders. Sam headed down the side-line and cut back, waiting for the long pass that was to come. The rest of the red squad set up some great screening as Tara sent a cross-field pass, which Steph picked off beautifully. The blue squad stormed after her. Steph faked a push pass, then sent a high punt toward Sam. Sam leapt into the air and hit the ball backward over her head in a fantastic bicycle kick. It was spectacular!

Steph ran past Sam, collected the ball and started for

the blue goal on a breakaway. The red midfielders and the blue defence followed.

Sam headed after the crowd of players chasing Steph downfield. They reached the penalty area and Sam saw the defence closing in.

As they charged, Steph grinned. Without breaking stride, she made a perfect pass to Sam, who launched it high over the heads of the blue defenders and into the net.

Everyone went wild! It was a slick set-up and a great goal. It hadn't been enough for the red squad to win, but it didn't matter. They'd shown Carly and her teammates that the blue squad didn't own the field.

"You were great, Sam," Tara said. "I haven't seen Carly so upset in a long time. She wants to be captain of the team and can't stand any competition." Tara shot Carly an icy look, then headed to the locker room.

Sam looked over at the blonde. The last remaining feather in her ponytail holder looked a little worse for wear, and the sweat on her face made her eye makeup greasy and uneven. She was frowning.

Sam steeled herself and walked over. "Good game, Carly," she began.

"As long as my team wins, it's always a good game." Carly was casually juggling a soccer ball between her feet when, suddenly, she launched it at Sam.

Sam trapped the ball with her foot, stopping it dead. "That's twice you've tried to peg me with the ball.

There had better not be a third time." Her voice was quiet, but rock steady when she spoke.

Carly shrugged. "I knew you could handle it. Besides, accidents happen on a soccer field." She grabbed her gym bag and headed in to change.

Sam watched her walk away, then went to gather her own gear.

"Hey, Samantha Aqsarniq Keyes."

Sam whirled and came face to face with Josh Carter. His eyes were a remarkable shade of blue that matched the Toronto Maple Leafs jersey he was wearing.

"It was great that you came out to the audition. To tell you the truth, we were getting a little nervous. It's pretty tough to do *Romeo Dude and Julie Baby* without a great leading lady."

Sam tried to absorb the compliment while thinking of some way to tell Josh she'd decided to quit the drama club. "Thanks for letting me try out, but actually …" Then she looked into his eyes and her brain turned soggy. "Actually, I'm thrilled to be in the play. I hope I don't let you down — I mean the cast down."

Thrilled? She hadn't meant to say that at all, but her mouth seemed to have a mind of its own. She knew then there was no way she could let Josh down.

"Hey, I didn't know you played for the Lions," he said, glancing at her dirty soccer uniform. "I'm here to interview Carly for the school paper. I'm the star reporter, which sounds great until you find out I'm the *only* reporter." He grinned and looked around. "Since Carly's not here, how about I interview the newest Lion?"

"Okay, sure, that would be really *neat*." Sam groaned inwardly. Another incredibly geeky word. She started to wipe her forehead, then remembered she'd smeared Vaseline across her eyebrows to keep the sweat out of her eyes. She must look like a real weirdo.

"You're new to the base. When did you move here?" Josh asked.

"I flew here from New Brunswick, my family did, I mean my mom did, got transferred, I mean." Sam licked her lips, her mouth suddenly dry. "She's with the Lord Strathcona's Horse, but she has a Leopard not a horse, of course."

Josh raised an eyebrow. "Ah, I think you lost me, Samantha. Care to try again?"

Sam was out of control. She took a deep breath and began again. "My mom was transferred from Gagetown and is here with the Lord Strathcona's Horse. She commands a Leopard C2 tank and I'm very proud of her."

Josh nodded agreement. "Tanks are cool. I'd love to drive one someday."

"Josh! How's my favourite paperboy?" Carly giggled, barging in between Sam and Josh.

Judging by Carly's fresh makeup and neatly brushed hair, Sam decided that the girl must be a quick-change artist. The feathers had disappeared and been replaced by a pale lilac scarf that perfectly matched her angora sweater.

"Why don't we go for burgers?" Carly asked. "I'm famished. We can do my interview while we're eating." And before Sam could say anything, Carly had linked her arm in Josh's and was steering him toward the mall across the street.

Sam wondered if Carly Gibson could possibly be a bigger pain in the butt. She couldn't believe what a goof she must have sounded like, babbling on about leopards and horses!

But her attention was soon drawn back to the bigger problem at hand. What she was going to do about her one-too-many extracurricular activities? She'd enjoyed soccer today, but now she wanted to act more than ever. She simply had to convince her parents that she could do both, which would be tough; Sam wasn't that smooth a talker.

Her mind flashed to an *inuksuk* she had called *Niugvaliruluit*, which means *that has legs*. This *inuksuk* would tell a hunter which direction to travel to get home safely. She desperately wished she had one now to show her the way.

Looking down at her new cleats, Sam wondered: what if she didn't try to talk them into letting her do drama as well as soccer? What if she showed them she could do both? What if they came to the opening night of *Romeo Dude and Julie Baby* thinking they were going just to watch another school play, but instead saw Sam's stunning stage debut?

Her marks were good and she was sure she could keep them up by studying a little more. She might have to stretch the truth to keep her acting a secret, but she'd come up with something. Her parents would be so proud of her — first a soccer star and now a stage star!

Sam's head swirled with the possibilities.

5 RIVALS

Sam had barely made it home from school the next day when the phone rang. She tossed her backpack into the hall and snatched the receiver from its cradle.

"Hello," she said. Nothing. "Hello?"

"This is Carly. We have a game against the Western Dragons on Saturday and you're going to play. The coach said to work with you. Meet me at the soccer field at seven o'clock." The phone went dead.

Sam looked at the receiver, frowned and gave Carly Gibson a promotion to "Class A" pain in the butt.

Sam was stretching when Carly arrived, wearing designer-label workout gear. The only thing that didn't coordinate was the tenser bandage wrapped tightly around her knee.

Carly wrinkled her nose at Sam's torn sweatpants and faded T-shirt with the worn-out words "Drink Milk, A Million Calves Can't Be Wrong!" emblazoned on the front. When she saw Sam's shoes her expression changed. "Those are great cleats! I noticed them at practice yesterday. I've wanted a pair forever!"

Carly's reaction was unexpected. "Ah, they were an early birthday present from my parents." Sam looked at the expensive shoes and then at Carly's cleats. They were okay, but nowhere near the quality of hers. "With a clothes budget like yours, you could get a new pair for every day of the week." Sam juggled the soccer ball on her knees.

"Actually, my mom buys me all these clothes. She's not enthusiastic about my soccer playing, so she compensates by making me a fashion queen the rest of the time." Carly grabbed the ball. "Come on, I'll go over the Lions' Secret Strategy for Sure Wins." She headed out onto the field with Sam right behind.

They practised for over two hours. "Let's run through the plays again," Carly said after they'd already done them a dozen times.

"I think I've got it, Carly. How about you try some of my favourite no-fail plays?" Sam asked.

Carly shrugged and nodded. "Show me your stuff."

Sam was impressed by how quickly Carly caught on, even though Carly was demanding and a real hardliner. Nothing but perfection was good enough. Neither girl wanted to show weakness by calling it quits so they practiced until nightfall.

"I guess you're ready for Saturday," Carly said, yanking off her soaked sweatband. She pulled on her warm-up jacket and zipped it up. "You've got the moves, I'll give you that."

"You really know your stuff, too. Me … I always use the first rule." Sam grinned.

Carly looked puzzled. "What rule?"

"You know, the first rule of being a great forward: Act dumb and play smart. That way the opposition never expects my cool moves."

As the two girls started for home, the streetlights came on. The air smelled fresh, like what the colour green would smell like if colours had smells, Sam thought. They walked in silence. Sam glanced over at Carly. She had a new respect for the annoying girl's abilities, and suspected her own soccer skills had surprised her new teammate.

★ ★ ★

"Did you hear Ms. Wondergirl giving orders?" Tara asked as they did their warm-up stretches near the field.

Sam was looking forward to her first real game wearing the green and gold uniform of the Lancaster Lions. She would play as number sixteen, which had been her old number with the Gagetown Beasts. She noticed the entire red squad from practice was with her, while Carly and her friends were over by the bench. "You mean Carly?" Sam remembered how Carly had told everyone to warm up, then meet for the coach's instructions.

"Who else?" Tara said bitterly.

"Carly can be hard to take at times, but she can really play soccer." Sam started over to where the coach waited with his clipboard.

"But we think you're great too, Sam." Tara grabbed her arm. "We've been talking." She indicated the other girls on the red squad. "We want you to be team captain. The coach said he would wait to see us play before he made any decisions. You're the only one here who is a match for Carly. Do us all a favour and tell the coach you want to be captain."

Sam was stunned. The other girls were nodding their heads.

"And you're p-p-pretty easy to get along with," Stephanie said. "S-so far," she added with a giggle.

"I just joined your team!" Sam shook her head. "I wouldn't feel right being captain. One of you should go to the coach if you want to stop Carly."

"None of us can play well enough," Tara said. "We don't want another season with Carly giving orders like she's the queen and we're her slaves."

Sam thought about this. It would be nice to put Miss Pain-in-the-Butt in her place, but it didn't seem right. She hadn't even played one game and they wanted her for captain? Crazy! Besides, now was not the time to worry about who wore the big "C." "Carly really wants the Lions to win and that's why she's …" Sam looked for the right word. "Demanding."

The game was close. Charlotte, the Lions' keeper, was solid, but the goalie for the Western Dragons was fast and had quick hands.

Sam's squad played well, but the biggest problem came when Carly and her friends had the ball. Sam had been in the open several times, but the girls on Carly's squad had refused to pass to her.

"Two can play at that game," Tara called, dodging around Kelly Brandt, a midfielder and friend of Carly's. Tara was in poor field position, and Sam could see the Dragon defence swarming her.

"Tara, over here!" she called. Tara fired a pass toward Sam with the outside of her foot.

Suddenly, Carly shot in between Sam and Tara intercepting the pass. Immediately, she drove for the net.

Sam cursed and sprinted after Carly, positioning herself to take the rebound off the keeper. The Dragon midfielders and their defence had also been thrown off, and were slow to chase Carly and Sam.

Sam made sure she was not offside as she lined up against the deepest fullback. Carly began her run at the goal, dribbling close to protect the ball. Suddenly, Tara ran past Carly and the defence, into the penalty area and ahead of the play.

The ref blew his whistle for the offside against the Lions. Sam could hear Carly fume as she handed the ball over for the indirect free kick. Sam knew it was going to be tough to regain possession.

Rivals

The two squads under Carly and Sam battled to regain the ball. Sam could see the Dragons trying to understand the Lions' strategy. She shook her head. If they only knew how determined the Lions were to beat not just the Dragons, but the opposing squad from their own team!

Finally, in the last minute of the game, Sam found herself in a skirmish close to the Dragons' goal. As she tried to keep the defence from poke-checking her off the ball, she had a split second glimpse of the keeper. She was out of position far enough that Sam might be able to put one away.

Timing her shot, Sam deked out the girl covering her, then hit the ball with the inside of her foot, running it through and continuing on, getting the most out of her momentum.

Wham! The ball struck home with awesome force. Lions win! Everyone jumped and yelled. Sam waved at her parents as the final whistle blew, pointed to her new shoes and grinned. Man, did she love soccer!

As the girls came off the field, the coach called them together for an announcement.

"I've been waiting two years for this." Carly said, as she moved in front of Sam, blocking her from the coach's view.

"You ladies were fabulous. As you know, I was waiting to make a decision on who would be captain until I'd seen you perform when the pressure's on," he began.

"Today you played the best soccer I've seen in a long time. I'm concerned that your two-squad system may not be good for the overall team, but as a *game strategy*, I'm willing to give it a try. However …" He tipped his head, so that he could see both Carly and Sam. "I want to remind everyone that in soccer, all players work together for the good of the entire team."

It was clear the coach was warning them not to split the team.

"Don't worry coach," Carly smiled. "Making sure the Lions win has always been my first priority."

The coach glanced around at the girls before continuing. They were all listening now. "Because of the high calibre of play they showed today, I've chosen *both* Carly and Sam as co-captains. They will share the responsibility — win or lose. Congratulations, ladies."

The girls on Sam's squad applauded loudly, slapping Sam on the back. Carly's squad also cheered.

Everyone was excited, except the two new captains.

6 MUD PIE

The next week was busy. Sam seemed to have more homework than usual. Coach Dearing scheduled practice after school on Wednesday and again Saturday morning. The first drama club rehearsal was Saturday afternoon. A crazy schedule like that could make it trickier to pull off her master plan of super soccer, astonishing acting, and marvellous marks.

Carly was still angry at having to share the big "C" with Sam and hardly spoke to her all week, although they were frequently at their lockers at the same time. Sam couldn't be angry with her — she'd have been ticked off too if some strange kid joined the team one week and was made co-captain the next.

"I called the seamstress today and the new away uniforms will be ready soon. To pay for them, I've decided to have the team bake sale on Saturday," Carly announced after Wednesday's practice. "The under-14 boys have a game, and there will be lots of people around. We'll sell out for sure! Everyone will head over right after practice. So remember girls, bake, bake, bake and sell, sell, sell!" Carly tossed her shining halo of hair back over her shoulders, then waltzed over to Coach Dearing.

The girls on Sam's squad looked at each other. "B-b-bake, bake, bake!" Steph mimicked.

"And sell, sell, sell!" Tara added.

Sam made a face. She didn't like being ordered around. "I can figure out the sell part, but what does she mean by 'bake?'" she asked.

"We're supposed to bake everything ourselves," Charlotte Dorn said.

"That's not going to happen. I don't cook." Sam shrugged. "I'm no good with my hands."

"Is that why you play soccer? So you don't have to use your hands?" Carly asked, as she returned from her discussion with the coach.

Sam had never met anyone who could get her so angry so fast. She was used to playing forward — not defence. Someone needed to put Miss Bossy in her place. "Actually, Carly, I play soccer because I'm *good* at it," she said, giving her own hair a dramatic toss. She tried not to wince as her neck cracked.

Carly shook her head. "Even you can make sugar cookies, Sam. This is supposed to be a team project. You're not going to let the team down are you, *Captain*?"

She thought of the drama practice that was also scheduled for Saturday afternoon. She would have to be quick at the bake sale if she were to get to rehearsal on time. "Absolutely not! My cookies and I will be there!" Sam announced, already wondering how to make cookies. How hard could it be?

★ ★ ★

Saturday's soccer practice was particularly gruelling. It had rained in the morning, so the field was slimy. By the time practice ended, the sun had burned off the morning clouds, but by then, everyone was covered in mud.

Sam's squad held off Carly's in several of the drills and nearly beat them in the scrimmage. During the last play of the game, Sam did a spectacular dive, saving a sure goal. It was then that she heard the sound of material ripping. Clambering to her feet, she surveyed the damage to her shorts. The seam had torn wide open and her underwear was hanging out for everyone to see. The whistle blew, ending practice. The team headed off the field and over to the bake table, wiping mud off as they went.

"Tara!" Sam whispered as she looked around for cover. "I can't be at the bake table."

"Why not, we're grungy too." Tara jerked her thumb at the table laden with cookies. "And it won't matter as long as the cookies are clean."

"No, you don't understand. I ripped my shorts."

Sam's face burned with embarassment as she showed her the torn uniform.

"You'll have to remember not to 'turn the other cheek' to the crowd." Tara snickered. "They probably wouldn't appreciate being mooned by a muddy soccer player."

Sam winced. "I can't sell cookies like this."

"Yes, you can." Tara insisted. "You're our captain and there's no way you can leave us here."

Steph walked over and surveyed the damage. "S-s-stay at the b-b-back and no one will notice."

The three girls moved over to the bake table. Sam squeezed between Tara and Steph so no one could see her torn uniform. The rest of the team was busy serving the customers milling around the table.

"Say what you will about Miss Bossy, but she called it on the number of people here." Sam looked at the crowd that was arriving for the boys' game, then checked her watch. "We should be able to sell out and be gone by one-thirty." This would give her plenty of time to run home, clean up and make it back to the school for her first rehearsal with Josh. Sam glanced around. "Speaking of Carly, where is she?"

"She had to run home and get something," Charlotte said. "But she said she'd be right back. What happened to your shorts?"

"Sort of like a car wreck. I had a skid, then a blowout," Sam answered. She tried pulling her top down with one hand as she unwrapped her cookies with the other.

The misshapen cookies were black around the edges, but moist in the middle. Maybe a little too moist, Sam decided when she poked one and her finger came out gooey. As she licked the uncooked dough off her fingers, she realized that it tasted bitter. This surprised her, since she hadn't added any salt. She'd followed the recipe carefully, except for substituting baking soda for baking powder.

A mangy-looking dog walked over and eyed the baked goods. Sam offered her disgusting cookie to the dog, who sniffed it, sneezed violently and began to lift his leg on the corner of the table. "Hey, cut that out!" Sam yelled, shooing the dog away.

"Look at that," Tara said, nodding toward the parking lot.

Sam looked over and was instantly annoyed. It was Carly, but she sure didn't look anything like the rest of the team. She had changed into a new, tailored uniform in the away colours of the Lancaster Lions. Her name was on the sleeve of the matching hoodie and, unbelievably, the word "Captain" was neatly embroidered below.

Sam looked past Carly and saw Josh walking toward them with a camera slung over his shoulder. She groaned and looked down at her grimy, torn outfit, then at her teammates. They all looked like something the cat coughed up.

"You girls did great!" Carly smiled as she surveyed the table.

"No thanks to you, Carly. It's a good thing we were here to staff the table while you went to get cleaned up," Tara said, glaring at her.

"I convinced Josh to put our bake sale picture in the paper, and it only seemed right to show where the proceeds are going. I wanted to surprise everyone with their new uniforms, but when my mom went to pick them up, mine was the only one finished." She smoothed the front of her hoodie and turned to greet Josh.

"Hello Lion ladies or is that lady Lions?" he said with a wide smile. "Talented on the soccer field and in the kitchen. How about a photograph for the school paper?"

"I think the captain should be in the front, don't you?" Carly asked, stepping forward.

Sam had been trying to make herself inconspicuous at the back of the crowd, not wanting Josh to see her.

"We have t-t-two c-captains," Steph volunteered, yanking on Sam's arm.

"No!" Sam hissed, but it was too late.

"Hey, Samantha Aqsarniq Keyes! I heard the good news and I agree. Both captains should be front and centre."

Sam felt her face burn as she was pushed to the front of the group.

"Whoa!" Josh said, noticing the gaping hole in her shorts. His cheeks turned beet red, but his eyes kept straying back to Sam's underwear.

Sam wished she could disappear. She looked helplessly at Josh. "Couldn't we do this some other time?"

"Ah, no, my editor wants it today," he said apologetically as he fumbled with his camera.

Sam wondered how she could get through this with the least amount of exposure. "Okay, front and centre it is." She moved next to Carly and put her arm around her co-captain. Carly tried to pull away, but Sam clutched onto her shoulder for dear life. "Now, the rest of you crowd around, *really* close." Everyone did as they were told. "Closer, closer, that's great. Say 'cheese!'"

Carly forced a smile and tried to stick her elbow into Sam's ribs. Sam guessed her co-captain wasn't too pleased at being robbed of the spotlight. Sam didn't care. She wasn't going to make her first appearance in the school paper with her boxers flapping in the breeze.

Josh snapped the picture and winked at Sam. She felt herself blushing. "That's it. Thank you, ladies. Oh, and don't worry Sam. I'll be sure to feature you as both co-captain and the newest Lion." He gathered his equipment and turned to leave. "Are these yours?" He picked up one of Sam's sad, soggy cookies.

Sam was about to warn him when he took a huge bite. The moment his brain registered what his mouth had done, he stopped chewing and his eyes went wide.

But instead of spitting it out — as some of Sam's previous customers had done — Josh swallowed, and gave Sam the thumbs-up sign. "Great!" he choked.

Sam noticed Josh discretely jam the rest of the cookie into his pocket as he fled.

Carly cursed under her breath. "That's just great. I've been working with this team for three years. You show up and now Josh is going to do an article about you?" She shook her head and went back to the bake table.

As the girls finished their last sales, Sam looked up to see her mom parking the car. She waved and Sam headed over, wondering what her mom could possibly want. It was close to Sam's rehearsal time, and she didn't want any delays.

"Hi, Paniq." Her mom leaned out of the window. "It looks like the bake sale was a success." She nodded at the nearly empty table. "I'm on my way to Jordan's wrestling competition and thought you'd like to come. Dad's there now."

Rehearsal was in less than a half-hour. "I'd like to, Mom, but I can't because ..." Sam searched frantically for an excuse. Just then, Carly walked by and Sam waved. "I'll catch up in a minute Carly. I have to talk to my mom first," she called cheerily.

Carly looked at her confusedly, then shrugged her shoulders and kept walking. Sam turned back to her mom. "I'm going over to Carly's for something to eat, then we were going to watch a DVD. Is that okay?"

Her mom gave Sam's grimy appearance her critical eye. "You can't go looking like that, Paniq. Clean up first. We'll see you at home later." She smiled, and Sam smiled back innocently.

That was easy.

7 NEW COACHES

Lying to her mother made Sam feel like the lowest form of life on the planet, but it was for a good cause. When her mom saw how well Sam handled everything, she'd realize her little Paniq was able to take part in as many extracurricular activities as she wanted!

The auditorium was humming when Sam arrived. She'd washed most of the mud off, but her hair was still damp and hung limply on her shoulders. She wished there had been time to put on her new makeup. Sam wanted to erase the image of a mud-caked, skinned-kneed jockette from Josh's mind, and replace it with the exotic and mysterious Samantha.

"Hey, quite a change," Josh said, leading Sam over to a group of students who were busily rehearsing their lines.

Sam suddenly felt shy, and that bugged her too. Why was she being such a dope? She'd been looking forward to this. But as Josh introduced her, the best Sam could mumble was "hello." She desperately searched for something witty to say. She should be able to talk to these kids without her stomach turning over like she was about to jump out of an airplane!

"Let's get started, people!" Mr. Bidwell called, clapping his hands. "Romeo Dude and Julie Baby, let's run over your opening lines. Places, everyone!"

Sam stood rooted to the ground, not knowing where to go or what to do. "That's your entrance cue, Samantha," the director said.

"Right!" Sam was shocked into moving. This was so hard. Walking down the stage and into the light, she was surprised when Josh stepped up beside her. Of course, he was Romeo Dude. She hadn't put that part together. She held her script in a vise-like grip, and beads of sweat popped out on her forehead. She thought of the Vaseline she smeared on during soccer to stop the drips and hoped that wouldn't be necessary here.

Josh walked over to the prop table and picked up two hats. Sam gasped when she saw the elaborate lady's hat. It was tall, pointed, and made out of pink satin with lots of white lace draping from the top. The man's hat was old-fashioned, made out of black velvet, and had a huge drooping feather running along one side. The feather was a shade of blue that perfectly matched Josh's eyes.

The moment he placed the hat on his head, Josh changed. He wasn't just *acting* the part; somehow, he *was* Romeo Dude! It was like magic.

"Fair damsel," he said.

Hesitantly, Sam took the elegant pink hat from Josh and placed it on her head. She felt the strange weight and straightened her posture for balance. The lace swirled around her face and she raised her chin so that the delicate fabric trailed gracefully down her back.

The same feeling she'd had when auditioning came over Sam — the wonderful freedom to be someone else. She suddenly became this other person, this Julie Baby. "Good squire," she began, curtsying to Josh. "Let the festivities begin!"

What an incredible experience! Her fear left her as it had so long ago when she'd pretended to be the mighty hunter alone on the tundra.

By the time rehearsal was over, everyone was raving about how great Josh and Sam were in bringing their characters to life. Sam was surprised when she found out that Sheldon, who referred to himself as the Official Cast Nerd, would play her understudy, the person who would fill in if she couldn't make the performance.

After rehearsal, Sam walked over to where Josh was putting away the props. "Guess who my understudy is?" she asked with an impish grin.

Josh looked puzzled. "Haven't got a clue."

"Sheldon Holmes!" Sam giggled.

Josh clutched his chest with both hands. "Be still my beating heart," he proclaimed loudly. "Zounds and forsooth fair lady, I beseech thee — *don't get sick*. I couldn't imagine trying to recite poetry to Sheldon." He finished packing the props away. "That was quite a performance today. I have one question for you, Ms. Aqsarniq Keyes. Are you sure you've never acted before?"

"Honest." Sam blushed. "This is my first time acting." Then, remembering the mighty hunter, she added, "But not my first time *pretending*. I'm not sure if there's a difference."

As Sam left the auditorium, she carefully stowed her script at the bottom of her backpack so no one at home would spot it.

★ ★ ★

Monday was a nightmare. It began the moment Sam walked into math class to find Mrs. Steele impatiently waiting for her students. This was a sure sign things weren't going to be a lot of fun. The large woman strode across the front of the classroom like an angry giant.

"*Settle!*" the foghorn voice commanded. "First, we will review the pop quiz you *attempted* last week." Sam didn't like the sound of this.

Her teacher thundered on. "I have never seen such dismal results from a Grade Seven class. This late in the year, I didn't expect any of you to have trouble with simple geometry." Her stern glare swept the room.

Sam slunk down in her seat. She knew Mrs. Steele

wasn't talking about her, but she didn't want to get singled out for her work, good or bad.

Everyone rewrote the quiz. Sam noticed Carly spent a lot of time picking at her pink nail polish, and wondered if this meant she'd scored incredibly high or spectacularly low. Once again, Carly looked like a mini-model in a V-neck top with lace detailing. Sam was sure she'd seen that exact outfit in *Teen Miss* last month.

The minutes limped by on broken legs until, finally, the bell rang. The classroom emptied quickly. Sam saw Tara and Carly heading for the door. She began to stuff her books into her backpack and was about to follow when the foghorn boomed.

"Ms. Carly Gibson, I want to speak with you!"

Sam jumped, knocking the remaining books off her desk. Quickly, she knelt to pick them up. Tara had disappeared. Smart girl, Sam thought. Mrs. Steele's voice was enough to give a kid the hiccups. She peeked over the edge of the desk.

"You, Ms. Gibson, scored abysmally low on this test. So low, in fact, that you stand a good chance of failing math." She shook her head, which made the skin on her neck roll like tidal waves of flesh.

Sam shuddered.

Mrs. Steele continued, "You are very near the edge, and I would hate to see your future academic *or athletic* career jeopardized."

The last part caught Carly's attention. She opened

her mouth, but nothing came out. She looked like a goldfish that had escaped its bowl.

The grim-faced teacher paused and tapped her pencil on the stack of marked papers. Sam saw so much red ink on the tests that they looked like they were bleeding.

"What do you mean my 'athletic career' could be jeopardized?" Carly's voice quavered a little.

"That should be obvious, my dear. It is school policy that if your grades are too low, you are prohibited from playing any sport, including soccer." She scowled and her black eyebrows met in the middle like a thick hairy rope.

Sam could hear Carly's breathing quicken. "I don't think making me cut soccer will be necessary, Mrs. Steele. I plan on bringing my math mark up." She gulped, then added, "A lot!"

"I hope so, Carly. You must get your priorities straight. School work comes first. Extra math would make a great difference to your final mark. If there is no significant improvement soon, we will dismiss you from the soccer team." She turned abruptly and started to erase the board.

Carly held her chin up as she left, but she looked worried. Sam quietly followed her out of the classroom.

8 TIME SQUEEZE

Time was moving quickly now. Sam spent every waking minute running from school to soccer practice, to rehearsal and then back to the field for a game. She'd hardly watched any television or e-mailed her friends back in New Brunswick. Sam wasn't worried; she had everything under control and was sure she could keep it that way.

The Lions were playing the Sheridan Badgers, and it was going to be a big game. Everyone was excited, and there was some buzz going around that, afterwards, Coach Dearing was going to make a huge announcement.

The Lions hit the field and, as usual, Sam's miniteam battled against the opposing team *and* Carly's girls at the same time. The two squads fought just as hard against each other as they did the Badgers, but the twisted strategy was paying off. They'd won their last five games.

"Over here! I'm in the clear, pass me the ball!" Sam called loudly. She knew the midfielder dribbling was a "Carly Girl" and there was no way she'd pass to Sam, but the Badger defence didn't know that. They swarmed Sam, who was in a perfect position, not that it mattered to the midfielder.

By the time they realized Sam wasn't the receiver, Carly had scooped the ball and streaked down the sideline. Two Badgers midfielders headed to intercept. Sam moved up between them. The goal was wide open in front of her.

She knew if she ran forward of the midfielders, but did not have possession of the ball, she would be offside. If Carly played smart, she'd pass Sam the ball and let her take the shot. Sam was deadly in close.

Sam decided to trust that Carly understood what she was doing and would pass her the ball. She sprinted past the midfielders toward the goal. Unbelievably, Carly tried to take the ball in herself. The ref blew the whistle, offside Lancaster Lions, *number sixteen*. The ball was turned over to the Badgers, who drove down the field and scored, moving them one up over the Lions.

Sam was furious at Carly. "What were you thinking? You should have passed to me!"

"You shouldn't have tried to grandstand!" Carly shot back. "Next time, stay back and go for the rebound, *if* there is one."

Several plays later, the Badgers again had control of the ball and Sam, still angry, charged in. The second the Badgers' striker connected with the ball, Sam was on her like glue. She tried every technique she knew to get the ball away. Faking the girl out, poke tackles, block tackles — nothing would shake the tough forward, until Sam remembered the basics. *Time your attack to strike between the ball carrier's touches.*

Sam used all her patience; timing was everything. Touch, touch and tackle! She had the ball and was turning toward the Badgers' goal, when disaster struck. She was wearing her old shoes because she'd left her soccer bag at rehearsal. As Sam started her turn, several cracked cleats suddenly broke, throwing her balance off and giving her ankle a painful twist. Instinctively, her arm shot out to regain her balance.

Unfortunately, the Badgers forward was in her way and Sam shoved her hard, knocking the girl down. Again the whistle blew, only this time the ref waved a yellow warning card at her. Sam cursed; she hated getting warnings. They signalled you either couldn't control your temper or didn't have enough skill to beat the opposition fairly. Her patience was used up, her ankle throbbed, and time had run out for the Lions.

The game ended with the Badgers winning 3–2. The goal they'd scored because of the offside turnover was the winner. Sam was in a rotten mood. If Carly had passed to her, Sam was sure she could have beaten the Badgers' keeper. Sam had spotted a flaw in the keeper's netminding: she never came far enough out of the net to cut down the angles. An aggressive striker could deke her out, creating a huge hole to shoot for, and that's exactly what Sam would have done. But that was all history now. Game over.

The team gathered around as Coach Dearing called them to attention. "Ladies," he began. "Despite today's loss, you are the best team in the league, and because I have so much faith in you, I've entered the Lions in the Alberta Invitational Soccer Match. The winners of this tournament will go to a special soccer camp this summer and train with professional coaches." Everyone started talking at once. "That's not all. There will be scouts at this camp who will choose players to join the Edmonton Selects. This will open many doors for the girls who make it, maybe even a pro career." He held up his hands for silence. "There is one catch."

Everyone was now listening intently.

"This will mean a lot of extra practices, paperwork and, most of all, commitment. There will be no free time for most of you, but it will be worth it. I believe the Lions can win this tournament."

The girls cheered, which turned into a chorus of "Lions! Lions! Lions!" led by Carly.

Sam considered what the coach had said. Wow! The Edmonton Selects were the best! Then reality hit. She was stretched to the limit already — how was she going to squeeze in the extra practices? So far, she'd balanced everything, but it hadn't been easy. If her family wasn't so busy getting settled in after the move, she'd have been caught by now for sure. Several times, she'd left rehearsal and almost run into Jordan and her dad after wrestling class. One thing was certain; she was not going to give up drama, even if she had to break every rule in the book.

9 HOT STUFF!

Coach Dearing was right about the workload. He had strategy sessions to brainstorm new plays, run drills and practice mock games. Added to this were all the registration forms. This tournament was going to be filmed, so special release forms had to be signed. Plus there were the regular games and practices. Sam was going crazy with it all.

One afternoon, Sam turned from her locker to see Josh approaching. Immediately her tongue tied itself into a knot. It seemed the only time she could talk easily to Josh was when she reading from a script. She desperately wished she could make him understand that she was actually an intelligent person!

"I have the new rehearsal schedule. As we get closer to the big night, we will be practically living on stage." He handed her a sheet of paper. "I know this will be hard on you — spending a lot more time with me — but try to be brave about it." His eyes twinkled.

Sam scanned the revised timetable. "Oh no," she

moaned, glancing at the dates. The extra rehearsals overlapped with her soccer practices. "This bites, big time!" Sam blurted out.

Josh seemed surprised, then anxious. "Hey, I was only kidding! I mean, yes, we'll be at rehearsal together, but if you don't like being around me, that's okay." His face flushed. "I won't bug you if I see you at school or anything."

Sam stared at him. If she didn't know better, she'd have thought he was worried about *her* not wanting to be with *him*! Could calm, cool, Josh be nervous underneath? As if. Who was she kidding? She shook her head. "No, Josh it's not you. I have a scheduling conflict, but I'll work it out."

Josh looked relieved, and then he winked at her, back to his old self. "Great! I'll see you at rehearsal!"

★ ★ ★

"Hey, Carly, I can't make it to practice after school. I have to …" Sam thought of all the excuses she'd given Carly recently. Since starting soccer and drama she had come up with some doozies. "I have to go to the dentist today. Could you tell the coach for me? Thanks."

Sam slammed her locker and headed to rehearsal before Carly could stop her. Being nearly late for a soccer game last Saturday made her realize how much time she spent on both activities. She simply couldn't be in two places at once. Coach Dearing had already spoken to her about missed practices. She'd come up with the dentist appointment as a cover.

"Sam, wait a minute. The coach needs your release forms ..." Sam heard Carly calling. Oh yeah, the forms. They were in her room somewhere. She'd look for them later.

★ ★ ★

Sam was late getting home from rehearsal. Everyone was sitting at the dinner table when she rushed in.

"Where have you been, young lady? This is the third time this week." Her dad's face was grim. "The wrestling club had a meet after school, and since Coach Dearing was watching the match, there couldn't have been any soccer."

Sam was going to say she was at practice, but that was out now. "Uh, I was at Carly's. She has a field behind her house where we can run drills." Sam had no idea where Carly lived, let alone if there was a field behind her house, but unless her parents checked, it wouldn't matter.

"Hey, speaking of Carly, have you seen the school paper this week?" Jordan was grinning and Sam knew that wasn't a good thing. "You two look like Beauty and the Beast. Guess who's the beast, Sam?" He brayed like a donkey and Sam clenched her jaw.

Soccer Star!

Jordan held up the paper. The bake sale photo was on the front page. Carly, gorgeous and crisp in her new uniform, looked like a poster girl for *World Soccer*, while Sam looked like a drowned rat. To think Josh had been on the other side of the camera! Sam groaned. The only good thing about the photo was that it distracted her parents from questioning Sam about her absences lately. The rest of dinner was taken up with talk about the upcoming soccer tournament.

★ ★ ★

The next day was going to be a big one at rehearsal. Everyone would be dressed in costume for the first time and, after that disastrous photo, Sam wanted to be the most beautiful Julie Baby ever. As soon as the bell rang, she grabbed her backpack and raced for the girls' washroom. Carly looked like she wanted to say something, but Sam deked past her.

Sam had been shopping and had spent her entire month's allowance. She bought a fake, hot pink braid that she pinned onto her own limp hair. The braid matched her new lipstick. Sam thought they looked very chic together.

Then Sam put on her makeup and added a pair of false eyelashes to make her eyes look bigger. And for the finishing touch, she took perfume out of her bag. The bottle said *Gypsy Rose* and Sam thought it smelled heavenly. She sprayed the scent on her wrists, added several more squirts into her hair for good measure, and then surveyed the new, improved Sam. She looked at least sixteen!

As she stood in the wings, Sam noticed everyone glancing at her and whispering. They had no idea this grown-up, confident Sam had been hiding inside that mousy little girl. She swept regally onto the stage. Her costume was right out of a magazine, a pink and white confection that would fit in at any prom. Sam started to recite her lines — perfectly, she thought. An annoying fly fluttered in front of her face and was hard to ignore, but she managed to perform despite it.

Josh seemed to be having difficulty remembering his lines whenever he looked at Sam. She decided he wasn't used to her new look. She had made sure the hot pink braid was displayed prominently, although her tall hat covered most of her hair. The stage light behind her head made the braid glow like a Hawaiian sunset. "… Hey Romeo Dude, it bites that you're leaving me! Catch you later," Sam recited.

She was interrupted by an awful wheezing sound from stage left, where Sheldon Holmes was watching the performance. "He's having an asthma attack! He's allergic to scents. Who's wearing cologne?" Mr. Bidwell, the director, sniffed then stared at Sam. "My God!" he exclaimed, rushing for the fire extinguisher.

Sam didn't think her perfume was that strong, but

come to think of it, people were staying away from her. Even Josh had been keeping his distance. Suddenly, Mr. Bidwell was standing in front of her, aiming the extinguisher directly at her!

"Wait! I can wash the perfume off!" Sam noticed smoke curling around her head. Her pink braid was on fire! She must have sprayed it with flammable perfume and stood too close to the light. Frantic, Sam batted at the braid, but it was too late. Mr. Bidwell pulled the pin and squirted her with the fire extinguisher, covering her in a cloud of white powder.

The chemicals stung Sam's eyes and tears immediately began to run down her cheeks. They made little furrows in the powder. "Ow. Ow! *Ow!*" she wailed, hoping her contacts weren't melting into her brain.

"Someone take her to the washroom, make sure the fire is out, then wash that stuff out of her eyes. Sheldon, are you okay?" the anxious director asked. Sheldon was busy sucking on his inhaler.

Sam shook her head, causing a small avalanche of powder to fall on the floor. "I'm sorry, Sheldon," she mumbled. "I didn't know you were allergic to *Gypsy Rose.*"

"It should be called *Gypsy Toes.* It smells like old sweaty socks!" Sheldon coughed and pointed at Sam. "You stink!" he croaked.

Josh guided Sam from the stage. He led her into the boys' washroom and over to the sink.

"Man, when you mess up, you don't fool around! No one's ever going to forget this rehearsal. What were you thinking?" Josh cranked on the faucet. "You'd better get that stuff out of your eyes."

His tone was so angry, Sam could have cried. But when she blinked, something weird happened to one of her eyes. She could barely lift her drooping eyelid. Then she realized what it was. The fly that had been annoying her all rehearsal had been one of her false eyelashes flapping in the breeze. Now it was coated in white powder and hanging down her cheek.

Josh reached out and pulled the dead thing from her eyelid. "Friend of yours?" he asked, holding it up.

Sam wished she were invisible. Instead, she drew herself up to her full height and plucked the eyelash from his hand. "Thank you. I can handle this from here!" Trying to maintain a shred of dignity, she washed her face, then walked over to a urinal and shook the powder from her clothes. "Are there taps on this thing or what?" she muttered.

"That's not a sink, that's a ..." Josh began, but Sam had had enough. Without a backward glance, she stomped out of the boys' washroom and ran smack into Carly Gibson.

10 DIRTY DEAL

"What the heck happened to you?" Carly asked, as she took in Sam's grubby appearance. "And what were you doing in the boys' washroom? Couldn't find the girls', or were you just sightseeing?" She folded her arms and waited, her head at that peculiar angle Sam referred to as the "guilt tilt": the one parents used when they busted you with your hand in the cookie jar.

She had the urge to punch Carly right in her perfect face, but after what had just happened, she didn't have it in her. "None of your business. Anyway, what are you doing here?" She tried to straighten her outfit and failed. It was too demolished.

First Carly looked guilty; then she became defensive. "If you must know, I was looking for you. Did you really think I'd keep swallowing those dopey excuses you've been throwing around? You've missed so many soccer practices to go to the dentist, I was starting to think your teeth must be rotting." She pointed to Sam's costume. "And what are you wearing? A prom dress?"

Carly's eyes dropped to the floor, following the trail of extinguisher powder that led back to the auditorium doors. A big sign read: "Quiet, Rehearsal in Progress!"

"*Oh! My! Gawd!* You're in the play! That's why you've been skipping soccer!" Carly's voice was getting louder and wilder. "You've been lying to the coach, the team and *me! Co-captain* my butt! Don't you know how important this tournament is? If you don't want to play soccer, you shouldn't have joined the team!"

Sam was sure Carly's shouting could be heard in the auditorium. "Shhh, will you be quiet! I do want to play soccer. It's not what you think." Just then, Josh hurried out of the washroom, dusting the last of the white powder off his hands.

"Sam! I'm glad you're still here. I'm sorry if I was a little harsh back there. I've been pulling a lot of late nights with the play and all the other stuff I have on the go. I guess I'm a bit cranky." He turned to Carly. "Did Samantha tell you about our big excitement? Who says theatre is boring!" He took Sam by the shoulders and checked her singed hair and red eyes. "Looks like you're okay." He smiled warmly and all Sam could do was nod her head and grin stupidly back. "Carly, could you help Samantha with her costume? She's been through a lot today." His voice was so sympathetic, Sam continued to nod idiotically.

Carly looked from Sam to Josh, then back to Sam again, a knowing expression on her face. "Sure, Josh.

I'm dying to find out what happened at *Samantha's rehearsal today!*" She glared at Sam. "Come on, we'll go to the *girls'* washroom."

After she returned the ruined dress to the prop department, Sam couldn't stand having Carly stare at her a minute longer. "Okay, okay, enough of the guilt! Come on, I'll explain while we walk home." She didn't feel like she had a choice. Carly had blown a big hole in her super-secret plan.

As they walked, Sam told her story. "… So you see, my parents won't let me play soccer and act in the play. I was sure I could do both and show them I'm able to handle my own life." She sighed. "It would have worked too, except for that stupid soccer tournament."

Carly glared at her. "It's not stupid. It's going to be great! And the Lions are going to win."

"The Lions could win without me. You're so good, if you combine our two squads, the team would be unstoppable." Sam flicked out her foot, snapping the top off a dandelion and sending it spinning onto the road.

Carly hesitated. "I'm not sure we could. We've never won so many games before, and the only thing different is you."

"What are you going to do now?" Sam asked.

Carly looked grim. "I have no choice. I'll have to tell the coach. The championship can't be jeopardized so you can set your hair on fire in some dumb play." Carly slid a sidelong glance at Sam. "Of course, if you stopped ditching practices, I could forget about this …" She waved vaguely in no particular direction. "Acting stuff."

Sam's stomach knotted. If Carly told the coach, he'd tell her parents and then Sam's life would go straight onto the compost heap. Sam realized skipping so many practices wasn't fair to the team, but she had to rehearse. Suddenly, she remembered the day she'd overheard Mrs. Steele scolding Carly about her failing math mark, telling her that she'd have to quit soccer if she didn't improve.

"I know a way we can both win. You've been having trouble with math lately." Carly looked at Sam in surprise. Sam explained, "I overheard the Dragon telling you that if your marks don't improve, you're off the team. What if I help you with math and, in exchange, you don't blab about my scheduling problem?"

Carly looked at Sam for a moment as though weighing everything in her mind. "Maybe that could work." Her foot shot out and another dandelion flew. This one went even farther than Sam's. "Actually, between soccer, math and my …" she hesitated, targeted another dandelion, then went on, "… my other stuff, I'm starting to feel a bit burnt out. I have to admit, extra math tutoring would help. But I would need something else from you."

Now it was Sam's turn to look suspiciously at Carly.

"Like what?" she asked. "I'm not quitting the play, so forget that."

Carly shook her head. "I didn't say you had to quit. What you have to do is help me win. I want to be picked for the Selects, and the first step is winning that tournament. But if we lose, the coach will want to find the weak link so he can fix it for next season. As co-captain, of course, I'd have to help him." She looked at Sam like a cat who had caught a mouse.

Sam sighed. "How am I supposed to help you win? Winning is a team event, not one player's responsibility."

Carly grinned. "Now you're catching on. After you tutor me in math, I'll fill you in on the soccer plays you missed because you were at the dentist again." She shook her head. "Honestly, if you're going to use such lame excuses, at least pick different ones."

Sam grimaced. Though it meant helping Carly, this plan could actually work. "You're on," she agreed.

Carly didn't stop there. "And now tell me about you and Josh. I saw the way you looked at him. Come on, come clean."

Sam instantly felt flustered. "There's nothing going on between Josh and me. He's just, just … a fellow actor!" She didn't know what to say. "Besides, what about all that sappy stuff *you* do when he's around? Anyone with eyes can see you want Josh for a boyfriend."

Carly's eyebrows shot up, surprised. "A boyfriend? Are you nuts?" She laughed, a clear tinkling sound. "Josh and I have known each other forever. Our parents have been stationed at the same bases since we were born. We live next door to each other, for crying out loud. He and his annoying brothers are nothing but pains."

Carly punched Sam gently on the shoulder chanting, "Sam and Josh, sitting in a tree, K-I-S-S-I-N-G!"

"Cut that out!" Sam said, her face crimson. But deep down she was relieved that Carly had been teasing Josh, not flirting with him.

The girls spent the rest of the way home discussing when they would get together to make their plan work. The traffic was heavy as they walked beside the main road. The base was always busy with trucks and troops hurrying here and there. Although the place was filled with strangers, they felt like family to Sam, because everyone was in the military. She felt better than she had in a long time. Having someone to talk to really helped.

★ ★ ★

For the next couple of days, the girls worked on their plan, starting with math lessons for Carly. Sam went over everything she could think of to help her co-captain understand what Mrs. Steele had been teaching them. Slowly, Carly seemed to catch on to some of the basics.

Sam was almost feeling relaxed as she walked to the library for their next tutoring session. Then she saw it — a huge poster on the library wall advertising the play. There, in bold black letters, were the words "*Romeo Dude and Julie Baby*". She rushed over and pulled the poster down. What if her dad or brother saw it? She breathed a sigh of relief when she saw that the advertisement made no mention of the actors' names. She was safe for now, but keeping her secret was turning out to be a lot of hard work.

That afternoon's tutoring session didn't go so well. "No, that's not going to work either," Sam advised, as Carly struggled with yet another math problem.

"You're the tutor, *tute* for crying out loud!" Carly crumpled her paper and threw it toward the wastebasket. "I'm sorry, Sam, but I'm exhausted. I'm not as good at juggling several careers as you are."

"Okay, try this." Sam patiently showed her the steps again. She had to admit Carly was no quitter. They'd been at these questions for over an hour.

"Wait a minute!" Carly chewed rapidly on her gum, and then a smile slowly replaced her frown. "I see what you're doing!" She grabbed Sam's pencil and frantically finished the question. "Ta-da!"

She pushed the paper to Sam, who looked it over and nodded. "Now you're catching on," she encouraged.

When they finally completed the assignment, Carly sat back, exhausted. "This doesn't seem so tough once you know how to do it. It's like jumping out of an airplane — once you're past that first step, everything else simply falls into place."

At that moment, Josh walked into the library and Carly began waving enthusiastically. "Josh, over here!"

Sam felt her pulse quicken as Josh walked to their table. Suddenly she felt shy sitting next to Carly, who again looked like a teen queen. Sam was back to wearing makeup, but this time she stuck to the basics — lipstick, eyeshadow and mascara. She'd tossed her false eyelashes in the boys' washroom garbage.

Sam was trying to think of a brilliant opening line to say to Josh, when she felt her left contact lens shift. She blinked one eye, trying to clear her vision, and was mortified when Josh winked back at her. "Glad to see you recovered from the rehearsal disaster, Samantha. I'm also happy to say that Sheldon's fine, too."

Sam sat there, frozen. She could feel her eyes tear up and blinked even harder to clear them.

"Sam's helping me with these math equations and doing an amazing job!" Carly kicked Sam under the table. "Right Sam?"

What was Carly doing, for crying out loud? By now, Sam's eyes were burning with tears. They were still sensitive from the fire extinguisher incident, and now her contact felt like it was slicing right through her eyeball. A tear slid down her face, and then the other eye started to drip. Carly chattered on about how smart Sam was and what a talented soccer player she was. At any other time, this praise would have been great, but all Sam wanted to do now was retreat to the girls' washroom and take her contacts out. She sniffed loudly.

"Do you feel okay?" Josh asked. "You look a little …" He searched for the right word.

Carly stared at Sam's tear-streaked face. "Oh, my! Ah, we were talking about the snorkel-nosed spotted whale in Bora Bora, which is now on the endangered list because it turned out the spots are actually some sort of rare disease, and it upset Sam to think of those poor whales …" Her voice trailed off. "Don't worry, Sam. A dab of ointment and I'm sure their skin will be cleared up in no time. Why don't you go freshen up." Carly was frantically nodding toward the girls' washroom.

Sam took her cue and scurried away. Walking into the washroom, she saw her reflection in the mirror and groaned. Her mascara had run down her face, making black lines like railway tracks. This was the final straw. Grabbing a paper towel, she angrily scrubbed every trace of makeup off her face. Then she rinsed her contacts, smoothed her hair back behind her ears and marched out of the washroom.

"Where's Josh?" she asked, her spirits sinking to a new low.

"He had to leave, but said he'd see you at rehearsal," Carly replied.

Sam sighed, then flopped into the chair next to Carly. "I'm such a loser. I always say the wrong thing and act so lame when he's around."

Carly looked at Sam's pink face and nodded. "Tomorrow's Saturday. Want to come to West Edmonton Mall with me after soccer practice?"

Sam couldn't figure out this super-friendly Carly, and her face must have betrayed her suspicion. "No tricks! Honest!" Carly held up three fingers in a Boy Scout salute. "I have another brilliant Carly solution for one of your problems."

Carly smiled innocently and Sam wondered what she was up to.

11 A WHOLE NEW GIRL

Sam showed up early for soccer practice on Saturday. She worked hard and was exhausted by the time they reached the cool-down.

"Carly has been unbelievable!" Tara whispered to Sam as they stretched. "Bossing everyone around and complaining about you always being away." She looked concerned. "Why have you been away so much?"

Sam was surprised Carly was still angry with her about ditching practices. Maybe Tara meant Carly used to complain, before the master plan they'd worked out. She thought quickly. "Oh, you know. Dentist appointments and stuff …"

"Dentist, huh? Which one?" Tara asked as she stretched.

The problem with living on the base was everyone knew everything — like the names of all the dentists. "Uh, who do you go to?" Sam asked.

"Dr. Blair, in the building over by the big Canex," Tara answered.

"Yeah, Dr. Blair, me too." Sam knew she had to change the subject. "Have you ever been to the teen drop-in at the Family Resource Centre?"

Tara shook her head. "My mom says I can go next year if we're still stationed here."

The girls talked about the activities available on the base, like swimming, karate, golf and all of the cadets corps. "Hey," said Sam, "since my mom's with the Lord Strathcona's Horse, I could join the Strathcona's Cadet Corps. I wonder if I'd get to wear a black beret like her." This idea was new, but Sam had always thought that commanding a tank like her mother would be cool, and cadets would be a great place to start. The problem was, cadets would mean another extracurricular activity and she wasn't going to go there!

"You ready to go?" Carly asked, bouncing up to Sam and Tara.

"Where?" Tara asked, a smile lighting her face.

"Sam and I are going to the West Edmonton Mall. Since there's no bus from the base, my mom said she'd drive us. Come on, Sam." Carly headed over to where her mom waited. "We can change on the way."

Sam thought of asking if Tara could come, but Carly was already too far ahead.

"Well, see ya," Sam said, as she turned to follow Carly. She noticed Tara's smile had changed to an angry scowl.

Soccer Star!

★ ★ ★

The West Edmonton Mall was a blast. Sam's mom had given her money to buy a new pair of jeans, but instead she bought a wonderful outfit from Carly's favourite store. The berry-coloured top and matching short plaid skirt were gorgeous.

"Wait till Josh sees you in that! You won't have to worry about saying the wrong thing. In fact, you won't have to say a word!" Carly exclaimed when Sam walked out of the dressing room.

Sam felt beautiful as she looked at herself in the mirror. After she destroyed her costume in the fire incident, Mr. Bidwell said she could wear street clothes for the performance, as long as she was in character with Julie Baby. This was definitely an outfit a princess would wear! She'd think of a good excuse to tell her mom.

Sam didn't stop at buying clothes. When Carly went to get her hair cut, they discovered the salon was having a two-for-one special. Carly insisted that Sam needed a new hairstyle to complete her transformation.

The stylist cut Sam's hair short and spikey. The effect was cute and feminine, or as the stylist said, sassy. She looked like a whole new girl. "Wow!" Sam stared in the mirror. "Wait till my family sees this!"

"Never mind your family. Wait till your leading man gets a look at you." Carly took her arm and led her out of the store. "One more thing and the picture's complete." She handed Sam a tiny pot of clear lip gloss. "As far as makeup goes, that's all you need." She laughed again. "I feel like a fairy godmother."

"Why do you care what Josh thinks of me?" Sam asked cautiously.

"I told you, Josh and I are buddies from way back. I think it would be great if he had a girlfriend. He talks too much and you can barely complete a sentence when he's around, so it's a match made in heaven." Carly steered Sam toward the parking lot. "Speaking of which, how can you act on stage with Josh if you go to mush whenever you're together?"

Sam thought about this for a moment. "I guess when I'm on stage, it's not really me. I'm Julie Baby — beautiful, confident, assured — all the things Samantha Aqsarniq Keyes isn't." She clutched the bag containing her beautiful outfit.

"Let me get this straight. You can go onstage in front of total strangers and be this whole other person with no problem, but when it's one-on-one with Josh, you crater?" Carly looked at her quizzically.

Sam shrugged. "Crazy, huh?"

Carly shook her head. "No, I was like that when I started ..." she broke off. "Well, when I began this other thing that I do. I found that pretending was the only way I could get through it. So I guess in your case, you'll have to pretend to be Julie Baby whenever you're around Josh — on stage or off."

Sam stopped in her tracks. It was as though a light bulb had blinked on. Of course! She would pretend to be Julie Baby and the confident girl from the stage could appear anywhere! "Carly, you're right! I can be Julie Baby whenever I want, not just on stage. This is huge!"

Sam was excited. She was looking forward to seeing Josh again soon.

★ ★ ★

They went back to Carly's for supper, and Sam was glad she didn't have to go home right away. She needed time to adjust to the new her. Carly's mom was thrilled with their purchases.

"You two look great. Sam, that outfit is wonderful with your new hairdo. I'd say it was a successful day at the mall." Mrs. Gibson was a beautiful woman with a picture-perfect face and pale blonde hair like her daughter's.

As they ate, Sam sat quietly and listened, but became especially interested when Mrs. Gibson said she used to be in television.

"Oh, yes. I was on a morning show. It had good ratings, but when I married into the military, I had to make a choice. And I know I made the right one." Her blue eyes twinkled as she smiled at her daughter. "Carly's dad is a captain with the 408 Tactical Helicopter Squadron."

94

"Don't you miss it?" Sam asked.

"Oh, television was an exciting life, but this life is also stimulating. Not having to get up at three-thirty in the morning to go to work makes it a lot easier to concentrate on my other interests. Then there's Carly's opera singing, which takes a lot of time."

Sam looked blankly at Mrs. Gibson, then her gaze shifted to Carly. "What opera singing?" she asked. Carly didn't answer.

"Didn't Carly tell you?" Mrs. Gibson went on enthusiastically. "She has a beautiful voice and sings with the Edmonton Junior Opera Society. Her voice coach thinks she could be the next Renée Fleming."

"Who?" Sam asked, now thoroughly confused.

"She's a young soprano with the most wonderful voice, dear. Carly has great potential." Mrs. Gibson continued eating while Sam tried to picture Carly on stage wearing Viking horns.

"Hey Sam, did you see Canada win the Under-19 Women's Series? If they keep playing like that, the U.S. is in trouble come cup time!" Carly was obviously trying to change the subject. "It was great!" she continued, then offered a blow-by-blow of all three games in the series.

Sam tried to switch her thinking to soccer, but her mind kept wandering back to something Carly had said. Singing must have been the reason Carly was having scheduling problems of her own. She said she understood about pretending to be someone you're not.

By the time she got home, Sam had a lot on her mind — shopping, her new hairdo and now Carly refusing to talk about her opera singing. There was something very strange about the way Carly had acted.

★ ★ ★

Sam's mom and dad stared at her before saying anything. Then there were suddenly a lot of questions.

"Paniq, what have you done to your hair?" her mom asked.

"I cut it." Sam knew that sounded lame, so she quickly added. "I didn't need any money. Carly got a two-for-one and her mom paid for hers."

"It's ..." her dad fumbled for the right word. "Short."

"Right Dad," Sam said. "But easy to care for, so it will be good for soccer." She knew this would get her dad on her side.

"I guess that's true." Her dad squinted at her, still not sure of his daughter's new look.

"Did you get your jeans?" her mom asked.

Sam took a deep breath. "Actually, I got something else. It's the coolest outfit you've ever seen. I love it." She opened her shopping bag and pulled out the berry-coloured top for her parents' inspection.

"Beautiful colour. It will look lovely on you, Paniq." Her mom smiled. "But I thought you desperately needed new jeans."

"I got something better." Sam took out the cute plaid skirt and held it up, admiring the gold accents woven into the fabric. "And I didn't need any extra money."

"Where's the rest of it?" her dad asked.

"What do you mean?" Sam asked. "It's a skirt. This is it."

"It's awfully short." Her mom's smile became a frown. "And you usually wear jeans. Whatever possessed you to buy such a skirt?"

Sam felt her elation dwindling. "I like it."

"But don't you think you'd get more wear out of new jeans? Maybe you should exchange the skirt for something more sensible."

Sam looked at the beautiful outfit. Maybe she had been silly to think she could transform herself into someone else with a new look. She folded the outfit and put it back in the bag. She could return it next weekend.

Later that night, Sam sat on her bed and looked in the mirror. She was still getting used to the girl who looked back.

Her *inuksuk* winked at her from the windowsill.

Suddenly Sam felt strong. She was a new person! And it had nothing to do with her hairdo or clothes. Hadn't she stood up to Carly both on and off the soccer field? Hadn't she landed the lead role in the play on her first try? Hadn't she been managing soccer, drama, *and* tutoring? Taking her skirt and top out of the bag, she hung them carefully up in her closet.

The girl who wore those clothes was brave, smart, and confident, and that girl was Samantha Aqsarniq Keyes!

12 SHOWTIME

"What's the matter?" Sam asked as she watched Carly practice a scoring drill. It involved some fancy footwork to lure the goalie over to the far edge of the goal crease, then kicking the ball into the other corner. Tricky to pull off, but no goalie would see it coming. "You've been doing that same pattern for forty minutes."

Carly's face was grim and concentration lines etched her forehead. "It's nothing. The Dragon called my mom about my math mark and I had to explain how we're working on it and not to worry." She sighed. "Mom said she understood, because math was never her strong point either, but she reminded me that if something has to go, it won't be my singing. She also said that she'll keep in touch with Mrs. Steele so she can 'stay in the loop.'"

Sam grinned. "Don't worry, Carly. I won't let that loop turn into a noose."

Carly didn't smile back, but snagged the soccer ball with her foot instead. "I need to get this right."

When Carly was finally satisfied with her performance, she joined Sam on the grass. Sam was concerned. "Carly, it was only a drill. Lighten up."

Carly took a long drink from her water bottle. "You don't get it, do you?" She tossed the bottle on the grass and lay back, one arm across her forehead. "Soccer is important."

"Yeah, soccer," Sam said. "A *fun sport.*" She stuck a piece of grass between her teeth.

"Maybe to you," Carly mumbled.

"Wait a minute. What's going on here? Are you that worried about your math mark?" Sam pulled Carly's arm away from her eyes.

"Remember when my mom told you about my singing?" Carly asked. "Singing isn't a hobby with me. My mom wants me to perform professionally. I have voice coaches. There's constant practicing and auditions. Mom says I shouldn't waste my time with soccer."

"I don't get it." Sam felt like Carly was trying to explain something important, but she couldn't understand what.

Carly sighed. "I *love* soccer Sam. I want to play in the big leagues, but my mom thinks I'm going to outgrow it or something. That's why we have to win the tournament on Sunday. It's my chance to get on the Selects and show what I can do. If I can impress the scouts, maybe I can convince my mom to take soccer seriously."

Sam suddenly understood why Carly acted so weird

when her mom praised her singing, why she drove the team and herself to the limit and why her soccer always had to be perfect. "It means that much to you? Is that why you were beating yourself into the ground with that last drill?"

Carly nodded glumly. "I have to get it right. I have to be the best."

Sam thought about this. "It's kind of like the problem I have with my parents. They don't think I can do both soccer and drama, but so far I've been pulling it off." She shrugged self-consciously. "With a little fancy footwork … Hey, maybe you'll grow up to be a rock star instead of an opera singer — would that be wasting your talent? Or you could be the most famous soccer player ever. Who knows, we're only thirteen! By next year we may be rocket scientists or bag ladies."

Carly raised an eyebrow. "Bag ladies, huh?"

"You know what I mean. Being young is for trying out stuff."

Sam hoped her parents would see it the same way when she explained why she was in a play on Saturday night and a soccer game on Sunday.

"Can I ask you a question?" Carly said.

"Shoot."

"When we first met, you complimented me on my 'nutmeg'. What's a nutmeg?"

Sam laughed at this unexpected question. "A 'meg? You know when you shoot a ball through someone's legs, especially *a boy's legs* ..." She grinned wickedly as comprehension dawned on Carly's face.

"I get it," Carly said, and started laughing too.

★ ★ ★

At school the next afternoon, Sam ran into Josh at the pop machine. "Hey, Samantha, how's my favourite actor?"

His smile was dazzling and she felt herself sliding into the old tongue-tied Sam, then stopped and thought about being Julie Baby — poised, confident and self-assured.

She straightened up and looked confidently at Josh. "Hi, Josh. I'm doing fine." She spoke calmly and slowly, without a trace of nervousness. "I'm excited about Saturday night. How are ticket sales?"

Josh bought her a juice then walked her to class. Sam wasn't sure her feet actually touched the floor, but she didn't care. At the classroom door, she gave him a smile that would melt an igloo. She was about to leave when he reached out and tentatively touched her hand. He seemed to be at a loss for words. This was a nice change!

"I — I like the way you look today." Sam could hear something odd in his voice, like he was trying to make conversation to keep her there. Was he unsure of what to say? It did sound like he was tripping over his tongue, the same way Sam always did — up until now. This was too incredible!

Then she had a dismal thought. Maybe he was putting her on. Had she done something stupid again? She kept the image of Julie Baby in her mind, then decided to make Julie Baby a mighty hunter, just for good measure. "I discovered the best look for me — no makeup."

"Samantha, you're pretty just the way you are. You don't need all that stuff." The tension eased and he winked at her, the old Josh back in form. "I've been meaning to ask you if we could go to a movie sometime?"

Suddenly speechless, Sam could only nod her head. Then she recovered her voice. "Sure," she said. "That would be nice."

"Great! I look forward to it!"

Sam watched Josh walk away. She could have kicked herself. All the times she'd dreamed of the perfect answer when a guy asked her out and the best she could say was, 'That would be nice.' *Lame! Lame! Super lame!*

★ ★ ★

Finally Saturday night arrived, and the family was off to see "Sam's friend Carly" in the drama club's production of *Romeo Dude and Julie Baby*. Sam had spun this story so her parents wouldn't suspect what was happening. Carly would meet them there, and then

Sam would put her plan into action.

"Carly Gibson's that hot-looking babe from your soccer team, right?" Jordan asked as he put another gob of gel into his hair.

Sam placed her hands on her hips and looked her big brother squarely in the eye. "*Hot-looking babe?* You must mean my *friend* and it's rude to talk about her like that." The moment she said it, Sam realized it was true: she and Carly had become friends.

Her brother was taken aback by the unusual forcefulness of Sam's voice. "Whatever," he shrugged. But Sam saw the flush on his face. She gave him a look. It was great not to be the embarrassed one for a change.

★ ★ ★

The theatre was buzzing with students, parents, and faculty, and Sam's nerves were on edge. She patted her backpack where she'd tucked away the beautiful outfit. Sam spotted Tara and her other Lions teammates scattered around the auditorium.

"I'm going to go wish Carly good luck," Sam said, and disappeared into the crowd before her parents could ask any questions. Backstage, Sam found Carly talking to Josh and Sheldon.

"Samantha, we were getting nervous," Josh said.

"No skunk juice tonight, right Samantha?" Sheldon asked, sniffing the air.

Sam grinned. "Just the honest to goodness me! Give me a couple of minutes to change." She grabbed Carly and hurried to the dressing room.

Sam removed her new clothes from her backpack. The skirt glittered with gold in the bright dressing-room lights. She felt wonderful when she surveyed the effect in the mirror. "One more thing." She took the tall, pointed hat down from the shelf.

"Wait a minute." Carly took off the long scarf she was wearing. "This colour exactly matches your outfit. It will look great!" She fastened the filmy material to the top of the tall hat and helped Sam secure the head-piece to her short hair. "Break a leg!" Carly laughed, waving as she left.

Sam smiled. The old expression went back to the days when people curtsied or bowed, "breaking a leg," after a super performance. She tried to calm the squadron of helicopters in her stomach as she hurried to the wings.

Mr. Bidwell was busy checking the actors' costumes and makeup before the curtain went up. He clapped his hands to get everyone's attention. "I know each one of you is going to have a stellar performance tonight." He smiled at the cast. "But the most important thing is to have fun. Even if you have a blank moment, remember, the show must go on. The other cast members will help you cover any mistakes."

Sam smiled at her fellow actors. She did feel like

they were all part of the same team, just like when she was playing soccer. She took a deep breath, and waited for her entrance cue.

Sam's heart pounded so loudly, she almost missed her cue. Then she walked gracefully onto the stage — calm, poised, and from the way Josh smiled at her, beautiful.

The play was a huge success. The cast had two curtain calls and the leads received a standing ovation. Sam was surprised when Mr. Bidwell handed her a beautiful bouquet of flowers. "You gave a wonderful performance," he said over the applause. "Well done!"

Josh hugged her, squeezing the bouquet between them. "I'm so proud of you, Samantha," he whispered.

Between the clapping, the flowers, and Josh's hug, Sam positively tingled. She wanted to say something wonderful to Josh to commemorate the moment, and even started conjuring up the image of Julie Baby, then caught herself. Julie Baby was a character, but *Samantha* was real; she'd made the character come to life. She'd made the magic happen. She would always carry the mighty hunter in her heart, but from now on, people were going to experience the real Samantha Aqsarniq Keyes — a star.

When the curtain finally came down for good, Sam slipped backstage, where the cast was congratulating each other on a job well done. She couldn't have been happier. Then she saw her parents walking toward her.

"We have to talk. Now!" her mom said in her tank

commander's voice. Her dad's face was stern.

"Hello Mr. and Mrs. Aqsarniq Keyes," Mr. Bidwell interrupted excitedly. "I'm Carl Bidwell, the director. Your daughter did a great job!" He smiled at Sam. "Samantha, each year, we send our most promising female actor to the Vancouver Summer Drama School, all expenses paid. We'd like you to be our candidate this year. Congratulations! This could be the start of something incredible for you." He wagged his finger at her. "I knew you had talent the second you read for me. I can give you more details about the drama school on Monday."

He left to congratulate the other cast members, leaving Sam alone with her parents. The Vancouver Summer Drama School! Everything was happening so fast, her head was whirling! She focused on her parents, and the stony look on their faces. "Let's talk over here." Sam guided them behind some scenery.

"First, we want to congratulate you on a wonderful performance. You were very good, Paniq." Her mom's voice was deadly calm, which was always worse than if she yelled right away. "Next, I want to know if you are planning on playing in the soccer tournament tomorrow afternoon?"

"Yes, of course I am," Sam wasn't sure where this was going.

"This surprises us as we thought we had an agreement — *one* extracurricular activity only."

Sam cleared her throat. "I can explain ..." She sounded so lame. Her parents waited. "I wanted to show you I could handle more than one activity without screwing up. I worked hard to make my acting a success."

Her mom shook her head. "I don't understand how you were able to do this without us finding out." Then her eyes lit up. "All those times you were supposed to be at Carly's practicing soccer, you were here. You *lied* to us."

Sam felt the helicopters take flight in her stomach, then promptly crash and burn. She knew this would never fall into the category of a little white lie. "Yes, I did. I messed up, but I wanted to surprise you with the play."

"And you knew if we found out about it, we'd make you give up one of the activities." Her mom's eyes were like black flint, but there was something else there, a sadness. "I'm disappointed in you, Paniq."

Sam didn't know what to say. She'd wanted to show her parents she was a responsible thirteen-year-old who could make the right decisions. Instead, she'd shown them she was willing to lie in order to get what she wanted.

And not only her parents, she'd told huge lies to her teammates who'd been in the audience tonight. Everyone would figure out where she'd been all those times she'd said she was at the dentist. "I'm sorry," she whispered, but she knew that no apology was big enough.

"We'll talk about this more at home. Go and change." Her dad's voice sounded disappointed, and that made Sam feel even worse.

Dejectedly, she did as she was told. Josh was waiting as she came out of the dressing room. One look at his face and Sam knew he'd overheard the conversation she'd had with her parents. She could have died of embarrassment.

Josh pulled her aside. "It took real guts to admit you screwed up, especially to your parents. If you ever need a sympathetic ear, you can call me." He handed her a slip of paper. "I hope you get to go to Vancouver. I've been chosen as the male actor to go to the drama school. We'd have a blast."

Sam looked at the paper, where Josh had scribbled his phone number, e-mail address and a lopsided little smiley face. She felt like she'd let the whole world down.

13 TOURNAMENT TROUBLES

Sunday morning dawned bright and clear. As they drove to the tournament, Sam thought about last night's disaster. She hoped she could redeem herself with her soccer skills. Her parents had admitted she was excellent on stage, so now it was important to show them how well she'd maintained her soccer at the same time.

The tournament was huge, with the best teams from all over Alberta participating. It was held at the University Sports Complex on six soccer fields. When they arrived, the complex was jammed with athletes, coaches, and fans. Sam's parents wished her luck as she left to find her team.

As she made her way through the crowd, Sam spotted Carly, who stood next to Coach Dearing.

"We've got a problem," Carly began, before Sam could say hello. "Three of our players are out today with food poisoning. Zoe and Caitlin from my squad and Rosa from yours are all sick from eating bad seafood last night. It's a disaster!"

"Man! Rotten timing or what?" Sam frowned. "Okay, so we're short three players and that leaves …" She mentally went over the remaining list.

The coach shook his head. "I know the two-squad system has worked for you girls up until now, but you'll have to throw that out and play as one team today."

Carly pursed her lips. "Except we've been practicing plays and defence strategies designed for two squads. We can't change now, not on game day."

Sam suddenly slapped Carly on the back. "You'll love this, coach. The answer is so simple and obvious. We can still play with two squads. We'll mix the two together! We're all Lions, so what does it matter if a girl plays for your mini-team or mine? I've got spare defenders and you've got a midfielder I need."

The coach checked his roster and nodded. "I agree with Sam. And it would be great for the team to shake up the two squads, get them used to playing with each other again."

"Let's do it!" Carly agreed, grinning.

Coach Dearing called the team over and explained the new strategy. The girls seemed unsure that it would work.

"Of course it will work," Carly said reassuringly. "The drills are the same for both squads."

"We'll just be playing with different teammates," Sam added. "But our goal is the same. The Lions are going to win this tournament!"

The coach reassigned the girls and sent them to change into their uniforms. The Lancaster Lions were going into battle.

★ ★ ★

The girls discussed the lineup changes as they headed for the locker room. Everyone knew the change in squads was for the good of the team.

"I guess your parents weren't too thrilled with your secret acting abilities, huh?" Carly asked, adjusting her shin guards. She and Sam were changing at the far end of the locker room, away from the rest of the girls.

Sam shook her head. "It wouldn't have been so bad if I hadn't lied to them." She looked down at the "C" on her uniform. "And speaking of that, I feel crummy about all my lying to the team, but I couldn't be in two places at once. I hope this is the end to my sneaking around. It's tough keeping my stories straight."

A locker door slammed, startling Sam and Carly. Tara stormed around the corner toward them. She yelled, "I wondered about all those times you missed practice!"

Sam took a deep breath and stepped toward Tara. "Yes, I screwed up, but I never wanted the team to suffer. I worked hard to make sure I played the best soccer I could. Carly kept me up to speed so I wouldn't hurt the team, and since we're here today, I'd say she did a great job."

Tara turned her glare from Sam to Carly. "And I suppose you covered for your newest bud? For two years I've tried to be your friend, Carly, but I guess I'm not in the same league as Sam."

"Tara, you and I *are* friends." Carly stepped forward and stood beside Sam. "But Sam is a good soccer player and the Lions are winners because of her."

"Right. You two deserve each other." Tara's voice was icy. "Hey, girls," Tara yelled. "Come over here. First, we're down three players, and now I've found out Sam lied to us so she could be in that stupid play last night. She's missed so many practices, how can she possibly know all the moves like we do? She may cost the Lions this tournament!"

The look of triumph on Tara's face frightened Sam. She looked around at her teammates. They were all staring at her and they all seemed angry. No one said a word.

"Is this t-t-true, Sam?" Stephanie Nimchuk finally asked, the disappointment obvious in her voice.

Sam didn't know what to say. She nodded.

"This is really crummy," Charlotte Dorn said, shaking her head. The other girls agreed with her, grumbling about loyalty and trust. Several moved over to stand beside Tara, their arms folded and their faces grim. Sam felt a stab of betrayal. Some of those girls were from her squad.

"Well, we don't want to play with a liar, right girls?"

said Tara. There was agreement from the group. "We worked hard preparing for today, and we don't want our chances jeopardized by some *part-timer*. You should leave, Sam."

Sam was speechless. She didn't know how to make everyone understand how important soccer was to her. The only reason she'd lied was so she could stay on the team.

Carly raised her hands. "Wait a minute. Yes, Sam ditched practices, but she made them up. I coached her myself on the plays she missed. She spent hours of her free time practicing. Furthermore, Sam is a Lion through and through. She wants to win this tournament as badly as you all do."

Sam sensed the mood of the girls wavering. She stepped up beside Carly and faced her teammates. "Tara's right, I did lie and now I want to apologize. I screwed up and I'm sorry. Carly is the true leader of the Lions. I don't deserve to be co-captain and I'm going to resign. If you can't forgive me, okay, but let's work together and win today — win for the Lions." There was a moment of silence, then Steph cleared her throat.

"Today the L-Lions are going to roar!" she said in a strong voice. "*All* the Lions!" The rest of the team was hesitant. Then the mood lifted and everyone cheered. "*Roar, Lions, Roar! Roar, Lions, R-r-r-r-oar!*"

Tara grabbed her equipment bag and headed out onto the field.

★ ★ ★

The day was long and full of good soccer. After some initial confusion, the Lions adjusted to their new squads. One by one, teams were eliminated until the final round was about to begin. The best two teams faced each other for the championship. Those teams were the Southgate Drillers and the Lancaster Lions. The girls had fought hard and were ready for the final game.

"This is where that two-squad strategy you've been using will be put to the ultimate test," Coach Dearing said. "I had my doubts in the beginning, but today you've all worked as a strong team and shown that the Lions deserve to win this tournament." The girls cheered.

With her parents watching in the stands, Sam felt strong as she took her position on the field. No one could fault her play today.

The Lions were fierce and their determination shone through. The two-squad system really threw the Drillers off. It sure wasn't in any coaching book. With the clock ticking down, the Lions found themselves up 2–1.

Suddenly, on a drive down the field, a pushy Driller forward intercepted Tara.

"Tara, over here!" Sam shouted. She had a clear window to receive the pass. Tara glared at her, then tried to outmanoeuvre the aggressive forward. The forward charged, stripped Tara of the ball and turned toward the Lions' net.

Sam saw the Lions defence drop back and close in, ready to stop the Drillers' drive. The rest of the Drillers sped forward into the battle. Carly put on a burst of speed and ran to join the Lions' defence.

"Sam, cover the other side!" Carly called. "There's a big hole!"

"Got it!" Sam had spotted the weak area and was already running to block the opening. A Drillers midfielder was moving up that side, and Sam suspected this player would actually take the ball in. She covered the girl tightly. With this plan gone, Sam watched the Drillers try to regroup for their drive to the goal.

Too late, Sam saw that the Drillers had duplicated the sneaky midfielder on the opposite side. The ball carrier was shielded, so the Lions' fullbacks couldn't see her foot turn to kick the ball to the player moving down the sidelines.

In a series of quick movements, the Drillers' forward lofted the ball to the player on the sidelines, who wound up and smoked one into the upper right corner of the net. A clean goal — the score was now tied 2–2.

Fighting hard, the Lions began pushing back into the Driller end, but there wasn't enough time. The horn sounded, ending the tied game.

Coach Dearing called the Lions over. The girls flopped onto the grass, exhaustion written on their faces. "Because today has already been a long one, the officials have decided to go straight to a shootout." He handed out bottles of water. "We need one more goal."

Sam looked at the sweaty, exhausted team. They were tired at the end of their game. She knew if they took the field with this defeated attitude they would lose. She thought of the stories her grandmother told of how Sam's ancestors faced terrible odds to survive in the frozen arctic, and of how they never quit, but worked together to make sure everyone made it through the six-month-long winter night.

Then Sam had an idea. She jumped to her feet. "We are so close to winning this, I can taste it. We need to play a 'mental game' now. Think back to this morning. We were so full of energy, nothing could stop us."

She thought of how she used to imagine she was the mighty hunter out on the tundra. "Pretend we're marooned up north on an ice floe and we have to hunt a huge polar bear to survive. It's him or us. Make your mind believe. We have to beat this bear — the Driller keeper. We can do it! We're the greatest hunters Nunavut has ever seen!"

The girls stared at her as though she was a lunatic. "'Pretending' is another word for lying, and we've had it with your lying, Sam," Tara said.

Sam's spirits slumped and an overwhelming tiredness began seeping into her bones. What was the use? No one would listen to her crazy idea.

Carly stood up. "You pretended to be Julie Baby and it gave you an edge with Josh, right?"

Sam nodded, hoping the others would see this could work. "Hey, the guy thinks I'm the hottest, or is it the *coolest* babe around."

The girls slowly got to their feet. Sam's heart sank. She'd lost them. Sam wondered if Tara thought she'd be the next co-captain of the Lions. But the girls walked past Tara and came over to where Sam and Carly stood.

"I can smell bear burgers for supper, Sam!" Charlotte giggled, and the other girls laughed.

They began to make-believe they were hunters. Some peered off into the distance as though searching for the terrible bear. Others pretended to pick up spears or bow and arrows. Soon everyone was jumping, crouching and whirling around with new-found energy, their tiredness forgotten in this outrageous new twist to their game.

Coach Dearing chose Tammy, Steph, Tara, Sam, and Carly to be in the shootout. The four mighty hunters and Tara, who didn't want anything to do with Sam's crazy game, prepared to take their shots.

Sam saw the Drillers were also showing signs of exhaustion. They were a good team, she thought to herself. Not good enough to win, but they tried hard.

The two teams faced each other on the sidelines, waiting for their turns. The Drillers won the toss and started the shootout. Sam held her breath as the first player ran up behind the penalty mark, where the ball sat waiting. Moving swiftly toward the ball, she kicked a high, right, lofting shot, missing badly. The ball sailed over the crossbar. In her nervousness, the Driller had miscalculated and kicked too high.

Then it was Tammy's turn. She had a powerful shot, but the Drillers' keeper caught the ball, ending the play. In turn, Charlotte Dorn, the Lions' keeper, batted the ball back out of the goal crease, stopping the next Drillers shooter.

Steph nodded at the rest of the team and took her position as the Drillers keeper got ready. Steph had a good run, but the keeper's hands were too fast. Fortunately, the next Drillers player also missed. She couldn't beat Charlotte's lightning moves. No score.

Tara prepared for her try. "Good luck," Sam said. She knew Tara could be an excellent finisher, and now was her turn to shine.

Tara ignored her and faced the waiting goalie. She ran straight at the ball then, with a great deke, made the goalie jump for a faked high right shot, while she fired left. It should have worked, except the goalie had the reflexes of a cat! In a spectacular move, she did a flying header and deflected the ball wide. The crowd cheered loudly.

Charlotte was able to beat the next Drillers player. Still no score. Sam could practically taste the tension in the stadium. She swallowed. It was her turn next. She had the power to win this tournament for the Lions.

Sam walked slowly to her starting point, then began running toward the waiting ball. Her heart was pounding and she could feel the sweat trickling down her back. She'd been saving a special, secret move. With this one, she made the ball start straight, then curve hard right, past the goalie and into the net. This fancy footwork had beaten a lot of other netminders. She desperately wanted it to beat this one.

As she closed in, Sam saw the gloved fingers of the keeper flexing as she picked her side. Sam increased her speed, faster … faster! Then she kicked with all her might. She flipped the ball with her instep, making it arc sideways.

The goalie watched the ball heading straight for her, figuring on an easy catch. Sam held her breath. The ball should cut right and blow past the goalie. What happened next made Sam stop dead in her tracks.

14 LOSERS AND WINNERS

Sam watched the ball as it veered right, as planned. It was headed straight for the back of the net.

Springing sideways, the goalie threw herself into the air. Her body twisted until her foot was pointing toward the path of the ball. Her foot shot out and snapped forward. It connected with the ball and fired it back past Sam.

This goalie was unbeatable! Sam shook her head. The Lions had one more chance to score ... so did the Drillers.

The Drillers' striker lined up on Charlotte, moved in quickly and kicked low and hard. Charlotte's foot flew out and punted the ball back, high over the player's head. It was a great save!

Carly grabbed Sam's arm. "I can't do this," she said in a frantic whisper.

"Yes, you can!" Sam answered confidently. "You're going to score not only the game winner, but also the tournament winner. The Lions are going to that camp!"

Carly's eyes were wild. "You don't understand. I explained to my mom what soccer meant to me. You know, like we talked about."

"So what's the problem?" Sam asked.

"I told her if we won this game, she had to consider soccer as a real goal for me. The bad part is, I said if we didn't make it I'd never complain again about being an opera singer or hound her to let me play soccer."

Sam whistled. "Wow, nothing like loading a little pressure on! Look, I tried being sneaky to get what I wanted and I got caught. You were honest with your mom, which was the right thing to do. You can be a star, right here, right now." She smiled reassuringly at Carly. "Why not use something entirely bold, something legal, but ..." she put her arm around her teammate's shoulder. "Shall we say, *slightly* sneaky." She quickly told Carly her idea for a sure-fire-beat-the-keeper goal.

Carly listened intently. "I'm not sure it's legal, but I like it!"

Sam shook her head. "Carly, this is not some wimpy sport for scaredy-cats — this is soccer! The Drillers' keeper is too good to try anything ordinary. You've got to go for the wild and wacky. You can do it!"

Carly nodded. "You're right. This girl is too good. I'll do it. I'm going to send the Lions to camp. I'm going to win this thing!"

The crowd was chanting as Carly took her place. "*Roar, Lions, Roar! Roar, Lions, Roar!*" Carly turned her attention to the keeper.

She went in slowly from the left, as though she couldn't decide what to do. Then, as she moved closer to the ball, she stumbled and almost tripped. Catching herself, Carly extended her arm and pointed at the far right goal post. The crowd yelled its approval as she sprinted the last few steps. The keeper reacted to her signal and shifted a fraction to the right. This was the critical move. Carly's foot flashed out and smacked the ball as hard as she could, straight for the left side of the goalmouth.

Too late, the goalie corrected her stance and lunged for the streaking ball. She was within a hair of deflecting it. But that hair was enough for the Lions. The ball sank into the back of the net as the crowd cheered and row after row of spectators leapt to their feet.

The cheer became a roar as the scoreboard flashed 3–2 for the Lions. Carly Gibson had won the tournament! Best of all, the Lions had won by playing as one tough, united team.

The Lions ran onto the field and congratulated Carly. Sam hugged her friend. "Nice play! Fanciest footwork I've ever seen!"

Carly looked so happy, Sam thought she might burst. "This is the start of my soccer dream! Thanks Sam. Teamwork really paid off."

Sam ruffled Carly's perfect blonde hair. "And you remembered the first rule of being a great forward."

Carly looked at Sam, confused, then together they yelled "*Act dumb and play smart!*"

As everyone came off the field, Sam saw her parents approach. She ran over to them. "We won! This means we're going to summer soccer camp!"

The coach was standing nearby. At Sam's words, he walked over to them. "Could I speak to you in private?" he asked, and Sam suddenly had a bad feeling. Something was wrong.

"I heard Sam say she'd be joining the Lions at the soccer camp. I'm afraid she won't be." His face was grim as he turned to Sam. "You never gave me your registration forms for the camp."

"But I can get them to you right away." Sam could have kicked herself for not doing the paperwork, but with everything else, it had slipped her mind.

The coach went on. "I might have been able to work around that, but it's been brought to my attention that you lied to the team about why you couldn't attend practice sessions. I have no tolerance for lying, Sam. If you'd come to me and explained … well, maybe …" He shook his head. "But as it is, you're not going to camp. Now if you'll excuse me, I have to get back to the team."

Sam was astounded. She had planned to explain about the lying, but someone had beaten her to the punch. Who told the coach she'd lied about the practices?

It was then that she noticed that Tara had been

watching the conversation intently. The redhead locked eyes with Sam, then turned and flounced away.

Sam waited for her parents to say something, to come to her defence and explain about the play, but they just stood there.

Finally her mom spoke. Her voice was low and sounded sad. "You lied to the coach too? Oh, Paniq, you have some serious problems. It was bad enough you lied to us about the play, but you also lied to your team, the coach, and heaven knows whom else! How do you expect anyone to trust you again?"

Sam toed the ground. Her mom was right — she'd lied to everyone close to her. She looked her mom in the eye. "I wanted to prove I could handle things. When I was younger, I had trouble fitting everything in, but I've changed. I was able to both act and play soccer while keeping my marks up. I've also been tutoring Carly in math and she's doing well." This was the truth. She'd also discovered a new friend in Carly, which was an added bonus.

"I know I should have told you about the play, but I was afraid, and then I thought it was a great opportunity to show you I could handle more responsibility. The play helped me to become a better me. I'm not Sam anymore, I'm *Samantha*. I thought you'd be pleased." She waited as her parents mulled this over. "I'm sorry I lied to you. From now on, I'll make my own choices and I won't lie to do it."

"Your marks have been decidedly better than your brother's," her dad agreed. "In fact, Jordan now must drop all but one of his extracurricular activities."

Sam wiped away the tears that had worked their way down the sides of her face.

Her mom's voice softened. "Maybe we should have given you a chance to try both activities. We only wanted to protect you from getting in over your head again. The fact that you have had so much success and helped a friend with her schoolwork says something. Growing up is not easy, nor is it always obvious, especially to people like your parents." There was a hint of a smile and Sam began to feel a tiny bit better.

"I want to make one thing clear, Paniq. Getting older brings not only privileges, but also responsibilities and consequences. The consequences that go with this are as follows. First and foremost, no more lying. Also, we will not talk to the coach to see if he can be persuaded to let you go to soccer camp. That is off the table. You will apologize to him for lying and tell him you would like to be on the team next year." She raised an eyebrow. "I'm assuming you want to be on the team?"

Sam nodded. "I love soccer and the Lions are the best team I've ever played with, but what about acting?"

"I'm coming to that." Her mom said. "Your father and I have made a decision. Despite your wonderful performance in the play, you cannot go to Vancouver for the drama school. You need to rebuild our trust in you before you can take a trip on your own."

Sam thought about the long summer stretching ahead of her with nothing to do but hang around the base.

"But," her mom went on. "I'm sure there are summer drama workshops offered here in Edmonton that you may want to attend. You would have to come up with the money yourself, but if you really want to go, you'll find a way. You seem to have developed a talent for making things happen."

Her dad smiled. "I had a paper route when I was younger. I bought my first motorbike with the money I earned."

Sam felt a weight lifted off her shoulders. Her mom was nodding in agreement with her dad. "I think she's old enough to handle an outside job."

Sam hugged her mom and dad. "You've got a deal! Wait and see what a great job I'll do. I'll start looking into the drama workshops right away, and I'll apologize to the coach and explain everything. Next year's team will be wicked."

Just then, Sam spotted Josh walking toward them. Her stomach still did crazy barrel rolls when she saw him, but now they made her feel great instead of nauseous. She wondered if he'd miss her in Vancouver.

"Way to go, Soccer Star!" Josh smiled at her warmly, then added a wink. "Great game. Congratulations!"

He had a strange-looking stick resting on his shoulder, which he handed to her. "Hey, Samantha, have you ever thought about playing lacrosse?"

Other books you'll enjoy in the Sports Stories series

Basketball

❏ *Fast Break* by Michael Coldwell

Moving from Toronto to small-town Nova Scotia was rough, but when Jeff makes the school basketball team he thinks things are looking up.

❏ *Camp All-Star* by Michael Coldwell

In this insider's view of a basketball camp, Jeff Lang encounters some unexpected challenges.

❏ *Nothing but Net* by Michael Coldwell

The Cape Breton Grizzly Bears prepare for an out-of-town basketball tournament they're sure to lose.

❏ *Slam Dunk* by Steven Barwin and Gabriel David Tick

In this sequel to *Roller Hockey Blues*, Mason Ashbury's basketball team adjusts to the arrival of some new players: girls.

❏ *Courage on the Line* by Cynthia Bates

After Amelie changes schools, she must confront difficult former teammates in an extramural match.

❏ *Free Throw* by Jacqueline Guest

Matthew Eagletail must adjust to a new school, a new team and a new father along with five pesky sisters.

❏ *Triple Threat* by Jacqueline Guest

Matthew's cyber-pal Free Throw comes to visit, and together they face a bully on the court.

❏ *Queen of the Court* by Michele Martin Bossley

What happens when the school's fashion queen winds up on the basketball court?

❏ *Shooting Star* by Cynthia Bates

Quyen is dealing with a troublesome teammate on her new basketball team, as well as trouble at home. Her parents seem haunted by something that happened in Vietnam.

❏ *Home Court Advantage* by Sandra Diersch

Debbie had given up hope of being adopted, until the Lowells came along. Things were looking up, until Debbie is accused of stealing from the team.

❏ *Rebound* by Adrienne Mercer

C.J.'s dream in life is to play on the national basketball team. But one day she wakes up in pain and can barely move her joints, much less be a star player.

❏ *Out of Bounds* by Sylvia Gunnery

Jay must switch schools after a house fire. He must either give up the basketball season or play alongside his rival at his new school.

❏ *Personal Best* by Sylvia Gunnery

Jay is struggling with his running skills at basketball camp but luckily for Jay, a new teammate and friend has figured out how to bring out how to bring out the best in people.

Figure Skating

❏ *A Stroke of Luck* by Kathryn Ellis

Strange accidents are stalking one of the skaters at the Millwood Arena.

❏ *The Winning Edge* by Michele Martin Bossley

Jennie wants more than anything to win a gruelling series of competitions, but is success worth losing her friends?

❏ *Leap of Faith* by Michele Martin Bossley

Amy wants to win at any cost, until an injury makes skating almost impossible. Will she go on?

❏ *Ice Dreams* by Beverly Scudamore

Twelve-year-old Maya is a talented figure skater, just as her mother was before she died four years ago. Despite pressure from her family to keep skating, Maya tries to pursue her passion for goaltending.

Gymnastics

❏ *The Perfect Gymnast* by Michele Martin Bossley

Abby's new friend has all the confidence she needs, but she also has a serious problem that nobody but Abby seems to know about.

Riding

❏ *A Way with Horses* by Peter McPhee

A young Alberta rider, invited to study show jumping at a posh local riding school, uncovers a secret.

❏ *Riding Scared* by Marion Crook

A reluctant new rider struggles to overcome her fear of horses.

❏ *Katie's Midnight Ride* by C. A. Forsyth

An ambitious barrel racer finds herself without a horse weeks before her biggest rodeo.

❏ *Glory Ride* by Tamara L. Williams

Chloe Anderson fights memories of a tragic fall for a place on the Ontario Young Riders Team.

❏ *Cutting It Close* by Marion Crook

In this novel about barrel racing, a young rider finds her horse is in trouble just as she's about to compete in an important event.

❏ *Shadow Ride* by Tamara L. Williams

Bronwen has to choose between competing aggressively for herself or helping out a teammate.

Soccer

❏ *Lizzie's Soccer Showdown* by John Danakas

When Lizzie asks why the boys and girls can't play together, she finds herself the new captain of the soccer team.

❏ *Alecia's Challenge* by Sandra Diersch

Thirteen-year-old Alecia has to cope with a new school, a new step-father, and friends who have suddenly discovered the opposite sex.

❏ *Shut-Out!* by Camilla Reghelini Rivers

David wants to play soccer more than anything, but will the new coach let him?

❏ *Offside!* by Sandra Diersch

Alecia has to confront a new girl who drives her teammates crazy.

❏ *Heads Up!* by Dawn Hunter and Karen Hunter

Do the Warriors really need a new, hot-shot player who skips practice?

❏ *Off the Wall* by Camilla Reghelini Rivers

Lizzie loves indoor soccer, and she's thrilled when her little sister gets into the sport. But when their teams are pitted against each other, Lizzie can only warn her sister to watch out.

❏ *Trapped!* by Michele Martin Bossley

There's a thief on Jane's soccer team, and everyone thinks it's her best friend, Ashley. Jane must find the true culprit to save both Ashley and the team's morale.

❏ *Miss Little's Losers* by Robert Rayner

The Brunswick Valley School soccer team haven't won a game all season long. When their coach resigns, the only person who will coach them is Miss Little … their former kindergarten teacher!

❏ *Corner Kick* by Bill Swan

A fierce rivalry erupts between Michael Strike, captain of both the school soccer and chess teams, and Zahir, a talented newcomer from the Middle East.

❏ *Just for Kicks* by Robert Rayner

When their parents begin taking their games too seriously, it's up to the soccer-mad gang from Brunswick Valley School to reclaim the spirit of their sport.

❏ *Play On* by Sandra Diersch

Alecia's soccer team is preparing for the championship game but their game is suffering as the players get distracted by other interests. Can they renew their commitment to their sport in order to make it to the finals?

❏ *Suspended* by Robert Rayner

The Brunswick Valley soccer form their own unofficial team after falling foul to the Principal's Code of Conduct. But will they be allowed to play in the championship game before they get discovered?

❏ *Foul Play* by Beverly Scudamore

Remy and Alison play on rival soccer teams. When Remy finds out Alison has a special plan to beat Remy's team in the tournament, she becomes convinced that Alison will sabotage her team's players

Swimming

❏ *Breathing Not Required* by Michele Martin Bossley

Gracie works so hard to be chosen for the solo at synchronized swimming that she almost loses her best friend in the process.

❏ *Water Fight!* by Michele Martin Bossley

Josie's perfect sister is driving her crazy, but when she takes up swimming — Josie's sport — it's too much to take.

❏ *Taking a Dive* by Michele Martin Bossley

Josie holds the provincial record for the butterfly, but in this sequel to *Water Fight!* she can't seem to match her own time and might not go on to the nationals.

❏ *Great Lengths* by Sandra Diersch

Fourteen-year-old Jessie decides to find out whether the rumours about a new swimmer at her Vancouver club are true.

❏ *Pool Princess* by Michele Martin Bossley

In this sequel to *Breathing Not Required*, Gracie must deal with a bully on the new synchro team in Calgary.

❏ *Flip Turn* by Monique Polak

When the family situation takes a grim turn, swimmer Victoria finds help — in and out of the pool — from the person she least expects.

❏ *False Start* by Sandra Diersch

Caitlynn makes a deal with her grandfather to join a swim team if he'll stay and watch all of her practices. But after Grandpa has a stroke, Caitlynn doesn't want to keep up her end of the deal.

Track and Field

❏ *Mikayla's Victory* by Cynthia Bates

Mikayla must compete against her friend if she wants to represent her school at an important track event.

❏ *Fast Finish* by Bill Swan

Noah is fast, so fast he can outrun anyone he knows, even the two tough kids who wait for him every day after school.

❏ *Walker's Runners* by Robert Rayner

Toby Morton hates gym. In fact, he doesn't run for anything — except the classroom door. Then Mr. Walker arrives and persuades Toby to join the running team.

❏ *Mud Run* by Bill Swan

No one in the S.T. Lovey Cross-Country Club is running with the pack, until the new coach demonstrates the value of teamwork.

❏ *Off Track* by Bill Swan

Twelve-year-old Tyler is stuck in summer school and banned from watching TV and playing computer games. His only diversion is training for a triathlon race ... except when it comes to the swimming requirement.

❏ *Mud Happens* by Bill Swan

Matt wants to change schools so he can be coached by the head of a team of elite runners. But is there such a thing as too much, too soon?